DANGEROUS JOURNEY HOME

Michael Hunter

DANGEROUS JOURNEY HOME

A Prodigal Son's Journey Back to Father God

Michael Hunter

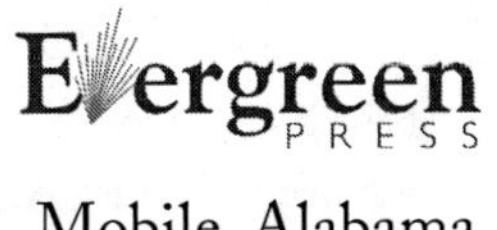

Mobile, Alabama

Dangerous Journey Home
by Michael Hunter

ISBN 978-1-58169-646-2
For Worldwide Distribution
Printed in the U.S.A.

Evergreen Press
P.O. Box 191540 • Mobile, AL 36619
800-367-8203

Contents

Author's Note

Please do not skip over the Bible quotations dispersed throughout this book. The Scriptures are not there to help support the opinions of this book. The purpose of this book is to help the reader become more familiar with the Word of God. We cannot learn to love God's Word if we do not read it. Many of the Scriptures have been taken from the *King James Version of the Bible*, because I have found it to generally be the most commonly available accurate translation of the original Hebrew and Greek manuscripts. I did keep in mind, however, that the *King James Version of the Bible* was written hundreds of years ago and contains many words and phrases that are now no longer in common usage. Therefore, for the purpose of clarity and ease of understanding, you will find that some passages are paraphrased (containing modern language) in order to help explain antiquated words and phrases. In doing this, every effort has been made to make certain that such paraphrases retain the integrity of the original Greek and Hebrew in order to ensure that nothing is added to or taken away from God's Word.

There are also numerous Bible quotations throughout this book that are taken from several different translations of the Bible, simply because I believe that they offer the clearest and most accurate modern-language translation of that particular passage, expressing the Word of God in a way that is easy for everyone to understand while maintaining the integrity of the original Hebrew and Greek Scriptures. Greek and Hebrew definitions have been sourced from *Strong's Exhaustive Concordance*.

Introduction

I was born in 1953, so I'm what the world refers to as a "baby boomer," a whole generation of people who grew up in the midst of a societal shift that started with parents who at least vaguely believed that there was a God. However, we were also born into a new educational system, which strongly taught that our parents were unlearned, superstitious, and misinformed about the origins of mankind.

World War II left an infected wound in the human race. Postwar society was complicated by the reality that many in my parents' generation were seriously messed up and unable to cope afterward. Although the term post-traumatic stress disorder had not yet been coined, many throughout the world were still struggling with PTSD as a result of the trauma that they had suffered during the war. My parents were no exception.

I grew up torn between two worlds. I loved my parents when they were sober, but I hated them when they were drunk—and they were drunk a lot. I despised conflict and fighting, but every year I got in trouble for fighting at school. I wanted to believe that God exists and that God loves us, but many times during my youth I cursed God because life seemed so unfair.

I tried to be a good person, but as life progressed I found that the evil in my own heart destroyed everything that I held dear. I lost my family, my wealth, my reputation, and my hope. I saw myself as a complete failure to both God and myself. In the end, I came under such condemnation that I began to struggle against a strong compulsion to kill myself—just to end the pain.

This is the story of how God reached out to me at the crossroads of death and how I finally realized who my true Father is and how much He loves me. It is also a wake-up call about a serious sin problem that is running rampant throughout Christianity during these last days.

Monetary crimes, substance abuse and addictions, adultery, premarital sex, child molestation, physical abuse and violence, even murder—there is not any sin that you can name without discovering that there are professing Christians somewhere who are mixed up in it. And the problem extends right up into the highest levels of Christian leadership and public ministries today.

There are those who believe that God is going to allow this sin-soaked Christianity to continue to exist in its present state right up until when Jesus Christ returns to set up His Kingdom on planet earth. They have forgotten that the primary reason Christianity exists today is that the nation of Israel was cut off from representing God because they too were an unrepentant nation.

I believe that we are now living in the midnight hour before Jesus returns to remove His bride from the earth. Jesus said that the wise will go with Him and the foolish will not. I pray that no professing Christian reading this book will end up in the situation where they are banging on heaven's closed door after Jesus catches up His bride, only to hear Jesus say, "I do not know you. Depart from Me, you evildoers, you workers of iniquity. You are appointed to suffer the tribulation with the unbelievers" (see Luke 13:27 NKJV).

The prophet Hosea declared, "My people are destroyed for lack of knowledge" (Hosea 4:6 KJV). The way to salvation that is preached throughout much of Christianity today is deficient, and it is destroying people. It is another gospel, and many are falling away because of it. It is time for Christian leaders to once again begin preaching the same Gospel that Jesus and His disciples preached. It is the only Gospel that will keep God's people safe on the path to salvation. The time for the preaching of repentance is now—before it is too late.

1

Family History

Victims of Collateral Damage

The truth is that World War II drastically altered human society. It was not until the late 1930s that the world began to grasp that Hitler's end goal for Nazism was total domination of planet earth. Young men and teenage boys, who were used to learning about life from their parents and their churches, were suddenly thrust into the reality of going off to war to fight and die for God and country. Back at home, their parents and siblings were not much better off either.

It was a time in history when children were required to grow up fast. My mother was a young Scottish girl of just fifteen when Great Britain declared war on Germany in 1939. With no men left to provide an income for her family, she was soon working alongside her two sisters with many other girls and women in the shipbuilding factories of Glasgow. There, Mom worked long, hard hours doing machine work and assembling parts for British battleships and destroyers.

Those were hard times, times of great suffering. Many people wondered if they would still be alive the next day. Sometimes they were too mentally, emotionally, and physically exhausted to even care anymore. I remember Mom telling me that the German bombers would come at night to bomb

London and then swing back over Scotland on their return to Germany. Any ordnance remaining was then dumped on any likely target in their flight path in order to lighten their load and give the German bombers the best chance to make it back home to Germany in one piece.

Live for Today! Tomorrow You Could Die . . .

Mom said that almost every night, the air-raid sirens would go off, and everyone was supposed to make their way to the shelters before the bombs started falling. Often, there was not enough advance warning, and many people never made it. Other times, they were so exhausted from their long hours at the factories that they just stayed in bed, choosing that, live or die, they were going to get some sleep that night before they had to go back to the factory to work the next day.

No one was untouched by the horror of the war. Fear, shock, pain, guilt, anger, sorrow, and remorse are all powerful forces. Not only were the lives of friends and family members who were soldiers lost in the war, but in our family all of my mom's teeth literally fell out from shock and anxiety when she was still a teenager. Mom's older sister's hair totally fell out and never grew back again. Auntie still wears a wig to this day.

By the time the war was finally over, the effect was more or less the same on the world population, regardless of whether people had been allies or enemies. An entire generation of human beings began to exhibit signs of post-traumatic stress disorder long before anyone actually identified the syndrome as a bona-fide disease. All kinds of physical and emotional problems started to come to the surface in people's lives, and our family was not immune from this experience.

This trauma of what people had seen and experienced

during the war, coupled with the threat of impending death looming over everyone's head, had also created a moral shift in many people's hearts, a determination to "live life to the fullest today, because tomorrow you could die." This philosophy, fueled by fear, became the driving force behind an altered social morality that is still thriving in the world today, and this change in morality came with its own serious consequences.

In the years during and after the war, the whole world saw a steady increase in incidences of premarital and extramarital sex in all its varied forms. People were increasingly turning to psychiatrists and drug dependency to help deal with their emotional problems (including addictions to tobacco, alcohol, and prescription pills, as well as illegal substances). Family violence and sexual abuse became rampant after the war, and it turned out that my family would be no exception.

Haunted by the Trauma of War: "Let's Get Away from It All"

Even though their hometowns were over five thousand miles apart, my mom had crossed paths and become intimate with a young Canadian soldier who looked past her toothless grin and wooed her with stories of the wide-open spaces, the peace, and the prosperity of Canada.

As soon as the war was over, they decided to do the right thing and get married, but serious problems began to emerge early in their marriage. Many people do not realize that about one in five women today will suffer the trauma of a miscarriage in their lifetime, and those numbers rose even more dramatically during the first decade after World War II.

Mom's first child, a girl, was stillborn, and this experience caused her to sink into a deep period of depression. Her husband began turning more and more to alcohol as he battled with his own traumatic memories of the war and his inability to help his wife recover from her depressed condition. Soon another child, a son, was born, but their marital dysfunction got worse instead of better after his birth. They survived on the hope that once Dad's European military service was over, they could return to Canada and start afresh. However, the truth is that changes in environment cannot permanently cure problems that are not primarily caused by one's environment.

New Country—More Problems

So it was that in 1951 my mother immigrated to Canada with her new husband and her young son, but life in Canada was far from the wonderful adventure that had been promised to her. Winters can be long and hard in Toronto, and it turned out that her husband was not as affluent as he had claimed to be. In fact, he was not well off at all. They were relegated to living in a small flat in the low-rent district of Toronto. Most of the little money they had left over after bills each month was being squandered on the bouts of drunkenness her husband used to try to cope with his PTSD, the result of the things that he had seen and done during the war.

Mom found work at a department store to help make ends meet, but that only led to bitter fights over how her paycheck should be spent. The situation started to get more abusive and violent. I often wondered about Mom's use of heavy makeup throughout most of her life. I eventually discovered that it was a habit that she had gotten into as a young woman, not so much to look nice, but to cover the bruises that were inflicted upon her face.

If you have ever thought that having children will solve your marriage problems, I assure you that most of the time it does not work out that way. With extra expenses and bills piling up, things began to get even more verbally abusive and physically violent for Mom at home. Finally, it all became too much. She was five thousand miles away from her friends and family with no one to help her, so Mom made a desperate decision. After a particularly brutal physical attack from Dad, she took her toddler and fled from her husband.

Even back in those days, Toronto was a pretty big city, and Mom managed to elude her husband for a while, eventually meeting another man named Bill who offered to love her and take care of her and her child, but more trouble was just around the corner.

Private Eyes and Kidnapping

What happened next was like something you would read about in a novel, yet it was very real. Mom was unaware that her husband had hired private detectives to hunt her down. They had instructions to find her—and then they were to look for an opportunity to grab the child and return him to his father, and that is exactly what happened.

Thinking that they were now safe, one day Mom and Bill left her son with a babysitter while they went out to dinner and a movie. While they were gone, a private detective showed up at their residence, bullied his way past the babysitter with legal threats, and kidnapped the child.

Mom was devastated. She went to the Canadian government for help, but because this was the early 1950s, there were no programs available to deal with spousal abuse and women's rights. The advice that she got from the Social Services department was that her husband was the child's father and "possession was nine-tenths of the law." If she wanted to have a relationship with her child, she should return to her husband, where she belonged. This recommendation came in spite of the fact that the authorities were aware that he had threatened to kill her if she ever showed her face around him again.

Mom told the authorities that she was too afraid of her husband to ever go back to him. Despite how ridiculous it sounds today, she was advised that the only other option she had was to look for an opportunity to steal the child back again, because once the baby was back in her possession, the government might then be in a position to help her, both financially and legally. Mom was too terrified of her husband to even try such a thing.

A Fresh Start, Another Child—Worse Problems

Eventually, Bill managed to convince Ella (my mom) to move west with him in search of a new life, so they began working their way toward the West Coast. When Ella found out that she was pregnant again, she contacted her husband one last time to ask for a divorce, so that she could marry Bill. He refused, and so it was that I was born as the illegitimate son of an unfortunate adulterous relationship. My middle name, Barry, originates from the circumstance of having the sudden onset of my birth occurring while my mom and dad were staying at the Barry Hotel in Saskatoon, Saskatchewan, in 1953. Mom never saw her first son again. I know that I have a half brother out there somewhere, but I have never met him.

After my birth, my parents continued their travels west, until finally settling in the tiny logging community of about 350 residents at Great Central Lake on Vancouver Island. I would like to tell you that things got better from then on, but they did not. My dad was more than twenty years older than my mom and in poor health. When she first met him, Mom did not realize that many years of Bill inhaling toxic fumes from his trade as a welder was contributing to his suffering increasing bouts of agonizing headaches, compounded by uncontrollable fits of rage and paranoia.

Soon Mom found out that she was again in the same situation that she had once escaped from in Toronto with her husband. Yes, Bill's was a different face, but the beatings were the same. As for me, I have little memory of my real father, other than an angry face accompanied by a hard-swung hand coming at me from across the kitchen table and then Mom doing her best to get between us to take the brunt of the beating. Mercifully, my father died suddenly of a stroke when I was just four years old, and Mom was once again free.

Religion Without the Compassion of Christ

I don't want you to get the idea that my parents were total admitted heathens. The war and the aftereffects of it had contributed a great deal to the breakup of families and to the ungodly societal atmosphere that continued after the war throughout most communities. In the early 1950s, most people in Canada believed in God, but (as is still the case today) there were many people then walking in various degrees of disobedience to the Word of God, not really knowing God the way that He wants us to know Him and follow Him. Nonetheless, most of the residents of small communities back then still attended church on Sundays.

I don't know what Bill's religious heritage was, but Mom's family was Presbyterian, so as far as she understood things, she was also a Presbyterian. It was not so much a personal choice, but a tradition in their home that was handed down through the family. On the other hand, it had not really mattered much to Mom and Dad that the one small church in Great Central Lake at the time was not Presbyterian. During the few years that they were residents there, they had attended the local church and contributed financially as they were able, just like most of the rest of the community did.

Aside from the cruel things about their unmarried state that were whispered behind their backs, my father's death was my family's first real exposure to formal religion that offered somewhat less than the compassion of Jesus toward hurting people.

When Bill died suddenly, Mom got to see the ugly side of religion. You see, this same church owned the only cemetery in the village. Upon Bill's death, church authorities told this bereaved mother with a four-year-old child that they would not preside over Bill's funeral or allow him to be buried in the cemetery because she had not been legally married to Bill. They did not want to defile the "holy ground" of their cemetery by burying a sinner there. Bill's attendance in church and his contributions to the offering plate had been welcome in spite of everyone being well-aware of their unmarried status, but ironically, the church drew the line at allowing his dead body to be placed in their holy cemetery.

In the end, Mom had to pay to have Bill's body shipped to the nearest town with a city-owned cemetery, where he was buried in a civil ceremony. It was the first of several bitter experiences that Mom would have with professing Christians over the years that were instrumental in forming a wall between her and salvation through Jesus Christ. It was a wall that would not be broken down until she saw the changes that God was making in my life—and that would not happen until she was sixty years old.

2

Alcoholism and Addictions

A New Father

Mom couldn't bear to stay in Great Central Lake after the experience with the church there, so she settled in the larger nearby town of Alberni, where she met a widower named Norm. They hit it off, and we all moved to Duncan a short time afterward. Norm owned a small two-bedroom house there that he had been renting out, and when the renter passed away, we moved in. I remember that my bedroom was so small that my parents decided to set up my bed in the closet to give me a little more room to play.

My stepdad, Norm, was generally a decent guy. He was a good worker, well-liked in the community, and I believe that he genuinely loved both me and my mother. I can honestly say that even though we were not wealthy, I always had food, clothes, and a roof over my head, but there were other problems in Norm and Ella's lives, serious problems.

Norm had never really gotten over losing his first wife. Losing her was really hard on him, and unfortunately Norm tried to block out those memories by drinking—and he drank a lot. Mostly, I think he drank himself into oblivion to try to cope with having lost his first wife at such a young age. Plus, it didn't help that he now had to deal with a spouse who had her own battles with depression whenever she reflected on losing two children, a husband, and a significant other.

Mom had never been much of a drinker up to this point, but she soon began to accept the philosophy of "if you can't beat them, join them," and it was not long before both she and Norm had a full-blown problem with alcohol. As for me, I was quickly becoming an emotional wreck before I even hit puberty.

Children: The Hidden Victims

One thing that the use of alcohol and drugs does is to dull a person's senses and warp their perceptions of reality, often making the users completely oblivious to the effects that their behavior is having on their family and friends. In case you did not realize it, let me explain that a closed door to a child's room cannot drown out the sounds of parents who curse and swear and fight like cats and dogs, repeatedly threatening to leave and split up the family. Children can hear what is going on even behind closed doors, and it is terrifying to them, traumatizing to them.

There were many days during my elementary school years when I was so burdened by what was going on at home that I could not get to sleep until the fighting stopped—and sometimes that was not until the early hours of the morning. In the early years of these occurrences, I was both frightened and hurt. Sometimes I blamed myself when they were fighting about me, but as I grew older, these feelings of fear gave way to anger, resentment, and rebellion.

During my teens, I actually wasn't much of a troublemaker. I wanted to be a good person, but if anyone tried to bully me, I would take all the rage and resentment that I felt toward my parents and vent it out upon the person who thought that the "skinny new kid" would be an easy target. And I never showed them any mercy. As far as I was concerned, they were at fault for attacking me and now they were going to pay for all of my suffering, including what I was enduring at home. I couldn't strike back at my parents, but I could certainly hurt the bullies at my school, and I didn't hold back if they pushed me too far.

I actually hated fighting and never was the one who started a fight. I wanted a peaceful existence, but the bullies seemed to think that this desire of mine was a sign of weakness. Every year for the first ten years of my schooling, I got the strap for fighting. In those days, corporal punishment still existed in the schools, and it did not matter to the principal who started the fight. Both of the fighting parties got the strap. It hardly seemed fair to me at the time—the same punishment for the aggressors and their targets—but that's the way it was.

Pornography: The Addiction No One Wants to Talk About

I was only eight years old when my best buddy who lived next door showed me a magazine with explicit sexual content. His older brother had smuggled it in from the United States, and the images and the sensations that they produced in me immediately changed my life. That one exposure to pornography was an emotional and spiritual seed that would quickly grow into an addiction to pornography that would last for decades and eventually contribute to the destruction of my own marriage.

Many people do not realize that the initial appeal of pornography is that it is pleasing and arousing to look at, but the demonic hook to pornography is that the release of emotional and sexual tensions associated with its use are addictive and totally self-serving. I soon found out that pornography and the activity that it stimulated gave me the emotional release and relaxation that I needed to get to sleep, even when my parents were in the midst of an all-out war in the next room.

I did not realize what was happening at first, but soon what had started out as an exciting new curiosity gradually grew into a highly addictive practice. Before long, I was not able to get to sleep without pornography and the emotional and sexual release that came with it. Furthermore, as is the case with many emotional and physical addictions, familiarity lessens the effect of pornography, so you are always on the hunt for a new and better high, always looking for something different, something more explicit, something more arousing—wherever you can find it.

A Victimless Crime?

It's a tragedy that pornography is such a forbidden topic of discussion in Christian circles because the sad truth is that many professing Christians struggle with an addiction to pornography today. This is partly because the Internet now makes it so easy to keep a porn addiction hidden from others within the darkness of people's own homes. But Satan also endeavors to silence our consciences by arguing that pornography is a harmless diversion, a victimless crime. Yet, pornography is not victimless—no, not at all!

To begin with, pornography changes the way that people view and think about other people. It prematurely draws young children into the realm of sexuality long before they are emotionally mature enough to manage such lustful desires. Pornography is also totally self-centered. Instead of stimulating your interest in other human beings as people, you become less interested in that and more fixated on what they might look like naked and how they can satisfy your own selfish sexual needs.

Is pornography victimless? Ask that question of some of the young children who have managed to get their hands on pornography and then become so overstimulated that they went to the next step of molesting their siblings or peers—and don't delude yourself about this fact. If you have pornography in your home, your children will find it and it will influence their thinking toward evil and ungodliness.

Since becoming a minister, I have counseled many people who are in the prison system. A huge number of men and woman are in prison right now for sexual crimes who will admit to you that pornography was present in their formative childhood years, and that it played a part in the development of their abnormal sexual appetites and eventually their sexual crimes. An addiction to pornography is never an excuse for sexual crime. An addiction to pornography does not absolve anyone of guilt or responsibility for what they do to other people. What pornography does do, however, is to influence some people toward sexual deviance in the same manner that alcohol can influence some people toward alcoholism.

Do you think pornography is harmless? Talk to the teens and single adults who find it almost impossible to relate to the opposite sex in a decent way because pornography is fueling their lust to the point that their primary goal in life has become getting someone else naked in order to have sex with them. They no longer care about people as human beings. They only care about satisfying their compulsion for sexual release.

If you think that pornography is not harmful, talk to the married men and women who have become so addicted and self-centered because of pornography and "marital aids" that they would rather relieve themselves artificially because it is quicker and easier than taking the time and making the effort to satisfy their spouses. Their spouses no longer arouse them anymore because of the influence of pornography on their hearts and minds.

What about pornography itself? Do you think that all of those pictures and videos were taken voluntarily? Talk to the children and men and women who are used and abused by the criminal element of society to produce pornographic materials. Many of them have been forced to do what they do. Others do so because it is the only way they know of to make enough money to support their drug addictions. Others are so emotionally and spiritually damaged that they do not believe they deserve a better life than to be used and abused by other people in the making of pornography.

Pornography is not a victimless crime! It is a gateway to abuse, emotional instability, spiritual damage, bodily injury, and disease, and even to physical abuse and death. Stop deceiving yourself. Godly sexuality is always love-centered and spouse-centered. Pornography and all other forms of sexual immorality are always self-centered, sin-centered, and demon-influenced. Pornography is one of the most insidious tools that Satan has at his disposal to prevent and pervert the beauty that God intended to occur between a husband and wife for as long as they both shall live.

People think that pornography can't be all that bad—but I tell you that it is. As far as a psychologically destructive substance, pornography is every bit as addictive as cigarettes, alcohol, cocaine, or heroin to certain people in our society today. I myself found out that once you realize that you are hooked and you try to stop, addicts to pornography experience the same tremors, emotional trauma, and sleeplessness that any other addicts suffer. If they can't buy it, serious addicts to pornography will even stoop to stealing it or raking through the trash dumpsters to get to it. That's how bad this addiction can become.

There is an evil spirit behind pornography, and it is one that is dedicated to destroying people's lives. Regardless of what type of addiction it is, all of them have demonic spiritual roots. All addictions are demonically engineered to destroy families in some manner. They can destroy physical and emotional health. They can destroy relationships, and they can destroy reputations. I did not realize it at the time, but even as an elementary-school student, I was headed down the road to being bound by numerous addictions that would all become instrumental in destroying my life later on as an adult.

3

I Don't Fit Anywhere

Geeks, Prudes, Jocks, and Hoods

Anyone who has ever been to high school is probably familiar with these clique titles, but in case you are not, I'll fill you in. When I went to school, if you were smart, you were a "geek." If you were religious, you were a "prude." If you were athletic, you were a "jock," and if you were overly ill-behaved, you were a "hood." There were also the "druggies," who were mostly composed of "hoods," but they often included members from the other groups, as well.

Finally, there was one other group, the one that I fit into, if you could call it fitting in. These were the "loners," aka the "weirdos." I was usually one of the new kids in school, because my stepdad had a habit of losing jobs due to his alcohol problem, and then we would have to move to another town and I would be forced to attend a different school.

I was smart enough to be a geek, but I was not willing to put in the effort to get the grades. In fact, ten years after dropping out of high school, I finished twelfth grade through the GED program with a ninety-six-percentile average. Then I successfully completed a MENSA exam, yet the achievement was not important enough to me for me to send MENSA the money they wanted to acknowledge me as a card-carrying member. Let's face it: I'm Scottish, so I was reluctant to part with a substantial amount of money for a piece of paper just to promote my own vanity.

I didn't fit in with the prudes, either, because even though Mom had taught me her vague concepts about God, Jesus, heaven, and hell, I had trouble reconciling those teachings with my pornography addiction and what we were being taught in school about evolution. I hadn't made up my mind about evolution yet, and my behavior tended to lean more toward that of the hoods than the prudes anyway, even if I didn't really identify much with them, either. So I wasn't interested in spending much time with religious fanatics (as the prudes were also called), and that kept me out of their circles.

I was actually athletic enough to win ribbons and medals in sports, but I was rarely motivated enough to put in the effort or commitment to make it happen. Sometimes a teacher would convince me to reluctantly go win a ribbon or two for the school if some team member failed to show up on sports day, but I much preferred to be out hiking or fishing or hunting—or getting drunk or stoned.

Truly, the group that I identified with the most was the hoods. They respected me because of my ability to fight, but I wasn't mean enough (or dumb enough) to want to become part of their inner circle. So I never really had many close friends when I was growing up. At each new school, I would end up seeking out one or two of the other "weirdos" who shared any of my common interests.

Girls, Sex, and Porn

I am certainly not very proud to admit that girls, sex, and porn were pretty much the whole focus of my activities during my teen and early adult years, but that's the way it was. My search for a sexual partner proved to be a big dilemma for me. When I was younger, my parents and the Bible both taught me that I should abstain from sex until I was married. Later on, the focus of my parents' advice shifted toward educating me about safe sex to make sure I didn't get someone pregnant. Of course, that conflict of values didn't do much to help me with my own inner moral struggles regarding right and wrong.

I wasn't looking for meaningless sexual encounters. I was actually a lonely young man looking for a lifelong commitment, someone with whom to share my life. I wanted to love and be loved in a way that my own parents didn't seem to be capable of, but that put me in conflict with my porn-fueled adolescent sex urges that were constantly driving me to try to get to the sexual aspect of the relationship before marriage.

My situation was not helped by the fact that I grew up in the abundant dope and free love era of late sixties and seventies, when birth control pills were becoming readily available and it was starting to be the thing to do for people to get high and try out different sexual partners to make sure that you were compatible before actually committing to marriage.

I am not going to give the devil any glory by going into any of the details of this time of my life. Suffice it to say that it did not take me long to learn that irrational decisions made while you are high on drugs and/or alcohol, combined with uncommitted, loveless sex, do nothing to bring fulfilment into your life. I never gave up looking for the right person to spend the rest of my life with, but porn continued to deeply influence my sexual appetites for ungodly behavior throughout my teens and early adulthood.

Motorcycles, Cars, and Guns

When I wasn't thinking about sex, I loved the sense of the open air, the freedom, and the certain amount of fearful respect that came with the black leather jacket and riding a loud and powerful motorcycle. I was never part of a gang, and I didn't want to be. I didn't like the idea of being vulnerable or having to answer to anybody else.

The same outlaw thinking carried over to my cars and trucks, as well. I was the guy with the 454-cubic-inch Chevelle convertible and the small box pickup with the Firebird 400 engine and transmission shoehorned into it, and my few friends also had similar vehicles. We would make a game out of roaring around town on weekends at high speeds until the cops started looking for us, and then we would just switch vehicles and do it all over again, partly ignorant and partly uncaring about the danger we were becoming to ourselves and the rest of society.

As far as guns went, I had a lot of them. I bought more than a few unregistered weapons from the back of someone's vehicle when I was still a teenager, and I always owned at least a few weapons. I even built my own working 40-caliber flintlock pistol. Gun laws and their enforcement were much more lenient back then. It was still illegal to carry a pistol around with you in town, yet I knew quite a few people who did that anyway.

Even before the movie *Dirty Harry* came out, it was not at all unusual for me and my buddies to go out riding or just walking around town with six-inch hunting knives hanging on our belts and magnum pistols hidden under our shirts, just in case we needed them. We were never looking for violence, but I was determined not to be a victim, so I was always prepared and capable of dealing with trouble if trouble ever came looking for me.

I was an expert marksman with a pistol, a rifle, and a bow. I could reliably shoot pennies stuck in a fence post from a distance of twenty yards, and I earned a silver medal in the Canadian archery championships when I was still in my teens. This included hitting targets up to one hundred yards away with a bow and arrow. As the new kid in high school, I would inevitably be tested by one of the local bullies, but it never took very long for word to get around that this guy was an armed biker with a violent temper when provoked. Usually one fight was all it took to establish my reputation.

The bad guys didn't like me much, but it was never my intention to be a part of their scene anyway. My motorcycle, guns, and violent reputation existed to send out a clear message that I was not someone whom you should be messing with. Just leave me alone. When someone didn't take the hint, a crazed look and some violently aggressive language was usually all it took to get them to back down. On the rare occasions that this was not enough of a deterrent, I would go after the attacker with such a vicious rage that it would frighten those who witnessed it, and the bully would never make the same mistake again.

Sometimes I really did want to kill the guy. I wanted to make him pay for all of the injustices that I had suffered growing up as a child, but somehow I always managed to stop short of using deadly force on anyone. It was like there was a voice in my head telling me to go ahead, while another Voice, which I now know was the voice of God, was saying, "Don't do it!" I guess, deep down, I really didn't want to hurt anyone. I just did not want to be hurt anymore myself.

Getting Drunk and Getting High

Some people think that growing up in a small town in

Canada would be pretty lame and tame, but that all depended on how you were raised and the people you knew. For the devoutly religious crowd and the law-abiding citizens, life was probably quieter, but we were the kids who were stealing booze from the fridge in our early teens while our parents partied it up in another room, too wasted to know what was going on.

This was also back in the days when bar owners were not as careful about checking IDs. Even though the legal drinking age at the time was twenty-one, I looked older than I was when I was a teenager. I'm also sure that many bartenders knew that we were underage, but I was still able to get into bars when I was just sixteen. As long as we didn't cause any trouble, we were rarely refused entrance or asked to leave. When it came to alcohol and drugs, though, the real action wasn't happening at the bars—it was at the private parties.

In smaller towns, most people are at least casually acquainted with others who run in similar circles as themselves. In pretty much any small town that I ever lived in, if you knew where to go, all you had to do was show up at a known party house with some dope or a six-pack of booze, and you were usually welcomed in to spend the rest of the night partying with whomever happened to be there—and pity the poor property owners the next day. Sometimes the damage was pretty extensive.

One thing I did avoid, however, was highly addictive illegal drugs. I was not so much against them from a moral standpoint, but I had seen far too many people in my life turned into walking zombies because of these drugs and I did not want to end up in the same condition. Nonetheless, there were still more than a few occasions when I got so wasted on booze and/or drugs that I would pass out completely.

I once woke up in the rafters of a barn with no idea of how I had gotten there. On another occasion, I called a friend to come and get me because I was too drunk to stand up, let alone drive home. He found me passed out in the snow underneath my truck in below-zero weather. Some would say that I am lucky to still be alive. I believe that it was God who continued to spare me from certain death over and over again, so that I would be able to write this book and teach others about God's long-suffering love and forgiveness toward mankind, including you and me, dear reader.

If you think that any of the things that I have told you about my life are more interesting or exciting than the life you might have led yourself, you need to get those ideas out of your head right now. I am deeply ashamed of the life that I led as a young man, and if I could do it all over again, I would have served God with all of my heart from the day that I was born. My years of sin and rebellion were a continuous source of pain and heartache for me, and I came close to death so many times as a teen and a young man that I know now that it was only by the grace of God that I survived all those years without becoming crippled or killed.

I am telling you my story in the hope that it will help some of you realize the foolishness of the life that I led, and that you would not make the same mistakes that I made. This book was also written to give hope to those who are already caught in the same or similar traps as the ones that almost destroyed my life. I don't ever want you to go the way I went. I am telling you my story to help you understand that it doesn't matter what you have done in the past, you can still change your life. You are not beyond saving if you really want to come to God. God does love you, and He can and will help you if you make the decision to repent (turn away) from your past sins and return to God, accepting Him as your true Father.

One of the things that you will need to learn in this life is that sometimes you are going to run into people who call themselves Christians, yet their lives are still full of sin. They do not accept or have not been taught that repentance (that is, turning away from all evil) is an integral and essential part of God's message of salvation for the human race through Jesus Christ. Please don't let that deter you from coming to God.

Their ungodly behavior does not mean that the Word of God is wrong or that Jesus is not our Savior. It only means that they are unlearned and in need of repentance and better teaching. Such evil human behavior and their evil beliefs are often the product of the evil seed that has been sown in their lives. It does not change the fact that God loves you deeply. I'm telling you that the Word of God is still powerful and well able to redeem all who come to Jesus Christ for mercy, forgiveness, and salvation.

4

Professing Christians

My Early Years and Religion

I already told you the story about the local church that banned my dad's dead body from their graveyard, but a few other memorable events took place during my childhood that turned my parents and me away from Christianity.

The first incident involved a large piece of property and the small two-bedroom house that my stepdad had owned. It was okay for Norm when he was single, but it was really too small to be comfortable for us as a family. Dad put the house and property up for sale, and we moved into a bigger house on the other side of town. After a while, Dad received a call from a man who asked if he could take a look at the house.

Norm agreed to meet them at the house and was greeted by a pleasant couple who maintained that they had just recently immigrated to Canada and were looking for an affordable place to purchase for their retirement years. They told Dad that this was just what they had been looking for, but they did not have a lot of money. They asked whether Dad could help them out by giving them a substantial discount off his asking price. Now, Norm may have had his faults, but he also had a soft spot for people in trouble. Even though our family needed the money and their offer was considerably lower than he wanted to accept, he sold them the property at the reduced price to help them out.

A few months later, we happened to be on that side of town, so Dad decided to drive by the house to see how the couple was doing. What he found was that the house was gone—and there was a big new church building that had been constructed on the property. Whoever was behind it all must have started building the thing right after they bought the property. Needless to say, Dad had more than a few things to say about that church—and they weren't very complimentary.

The next negative experience we had with people who claimed to be Christians came in the form of renters. The first was a family who were renting a trailer that Dad owned. After a couple of missed rent payments, Dad stopped by to see what was going on. What he found was that they had not only skipped town, but they had actually taken Dad's trailer with them, never to be seen again.

Later on, Dad rented out another house to a couple who were supposed to be Christians. They did so much damage to the house and property before skipping out, owing three months' rent, that Dad had to sell everything at a loss, because he could not afford to make the thousands of dollars in repairs that were necessary to fix the house up again.

As with many would-be Christians, Mom and Dad liked the idea of God and Jesus and Christianity, but they eventually got to the place in their experiences with "Christians" that they stopped attending church and did not want to have anything to do anymore with those who called themselves believers in Christ.

Sunday School and Boy Scouts

When you consider some of their bad experiences with

people who called themselves Christians, I was surprised when my parents did let me go off to Sunday school with one of the neighborhood kids when I was invited, but they never went to church themselves unless it was a Christmas or Easter pageant that I was part of. Mom and Dad also considered the Cub and Boy Scouts to be somewhat of a Christian-based, wholesome organization, so when one of my friends encouraged me to join the Scouts, my parents supported my desire to go with my friend.

I enjoyed Sunday school and the Cubs and Boy Scouts when I was younger, but eventually I quit everything after one too many ordeals of cursing and crying in the dark on the steps of the scouting hall long after everyone else had gone home. Unfortunately Mom and Dad developed a habit of going to the bar while I was at Cubs and Boy Scouts. They would lose track of time, showing up late and absolutely bombed, to drive me home. This was usually followed by their fighting all night about the whole incident while I tried to get to sleep.

Eventually I couldn't take it anymore, and I told them that I was no longer interested in going to Scouts. Parents have no idea of the trauma and confusion that their children experience when they tell them in the daytime that God and Jesus loves them, but then spend several nights a week after the sun goes down cursing and swearing at each other, physically abusing one another, and threatening to leave the family and never come back.

Reading the Bible and Ranting at God

In my later teen years, Mom gave me her cherished copy of the *King James Bible* after Norm threatened to tear it up in a drunken rage. Sometimes I would read it, wondering whether the stories in it were actually true. Some parts were boring, but other parts were quite interesting to me, particularly the parts about Jesus, who was not much like any of the Christians whom I had ever met.

Sometimes when I was going through a particularly rough time at home, I would pray to the ceiling, hoping there was a God somewhere up there who cared enough to listen and who was willing to do something to help my family. At other times, I would find a secluded place in the woods to curse and swear at God. I would shake my fist in the air, waving it at God and challenging Him to reveal Himself to me if He wanted me to believe in Him.

I never heard God say anything during these temper tantrums of mine; but strangely enough, they calmed me down, and I would come away feeling better, as if God had somehow heard and understood my frustration, even if He was not going to answer me directly or do anything about my family situation.

1972—Death Comes Knocking

I was nineteen years old, returning home to accept a job offer after being on my own away from Mom and Dad since I had turned seventeen. I had just bought a souped-up Chevelle two weeks before, and I was pushing it to the limit on the way home. I was about five hundred miles into a seven-hundred-mile trip, and I was almost flying, averaging over a hundred miles an hour whenever traffic allowed.

When I soared over the crest of a hill while coming down into the town of Quesnel, I immediately became angry because I could see that I was going to have to slow down due to the heavy traffic near the town. I had to drop my speed to about fifty miles per hour, and I was blocked in by traffic on all sides when suddenly it happened. Someone in a three-quarter-ton truck waiting to turn left across the highway was momentarily blinded by the sun setting behind my vehicle. They did not see my car, and they turned head-on right into me. It was all over before I even had time to move my foot from the gas pedal to the brakes.

My car careened off their truck into a steel lamppost, and all of my belongings that had been stacked in the back of the car came pouring over the seat backs, helping to pin me in the driver's seat. Passersby quickly came and helped to extricate me from the vehicle. The police and ambulance must have been close by, as well, because they were there almost immediately.

The policeman checked me over, asking me to sit on the curb and wait for him to help the ambulance attendants provide medical assistance to the other people who had been involved in the crash. The people in the other vehicle were quite seriously injured and would need to be taken to the hospital right away. The policeman told me that when he was finished, he would return to take me to the hospital. I sat on the curb for a while and then tried to stand, but every time I tried to stand up to see what was going on, I became dizzy and had to sit down again.

Finally, the policeman returned and offered to help me into his car for the trip to the hospital. At first I protested a little, saying that I was just a bit dizzy and didn't think that I needed to go to the hospital. But the policeman explained that I was bleeding, and he pointed to my chest. When I looked down to see that my chest was covered in blood, I realized that I was dizzy because my chin had been split wide open and that I had suffered a pretty serious concussion.

At the hospital, they stitched me up and kept me overnight for observation. The next day I was given a clean bill of health and told that I was okay to go. I never realized how serious the whole thing was until I went back to retrieve my belongings from my car the next day.

5

Did I Hear?

Examining the Wreckage

The following day, after the accident, I talked with the police department and the insurance company. They assured me that there were plenty of witnesses who had testified that the other driver was at fault, and that their insurance was going to cover all of my costs, including the cost of a replacement vehicle and wages from any lost time from work. Later on, I went to the wreckers to retrieve my belongings from the car. Then and only then did it dawn on me how close to death I had actually come.

The people in the other vehicle had suffered broken limbs, broken ribs, and smashed faces. I had not been wearing a seat belt, yet aside from six stitches in my chin and a little soreness in my thumbs, I had come through the accident relatively unscathed. Consequently, I was pretty unnerved when I took my first look at the car. The headlights were just outside of the broken windshield, the motor was pushed up through the floor, and both front doors had buckled so badly that they wouldn't even come close to closing.

When I saw the steering wheel, I realized why my thumbs were so sore—I had bent the steering wheel completely in half. I knew then that—without a seat belt—if either my thumbs or the steering wheel had broken, my chest would have been crushed by the steering column, or my body could have even gone through the windshield. The most disturbing thought came to me when I remembered that less than sixty seconds before the accident, I had been traveling at over 100 miles an hour. It was obvious to me that if I had hit the other vehicle at that speed, everyone involved would have almost certainly have been killed, and that's when I heard the voice.

God Does Speak to Us

As I was thinking about the events that had just transpired and how close I had come to dying, I clearly heard someone say to me, "If not for Me, you would be dead." It was so clear that I turned my head to see who was talking to me, but there was no one there. It was then that I realized I had not heard the voice with my physical ears, but with my spirit, and at that moment in my life God suddenly became real to me.

I know there are those who would suggest that I just imagined hearing a voice, or that I only heard it because I wanted to hear it. Yet I was not at all a particularly religious person at that point in my life. I was not even thinking about God at the time. I was merely contemplating how close I had come to death. Yet I know what I heard—and it instantly changed my life. What I heard started me on a nine-year journey of trying to understand and learn everything I could about this God who had spoken to me so clearly.

Choosing a Religion

For once in my life, I finally had a goal and a purpose: I wanted to find out about God. That was the day that sealed things for me in the argument between belief in God and belief in atheism. For me, ever since 1972, the score has been God: 1 and atheism: 0. God wins! The next big challenge was for me to decide which religion, or belief in God, was the closest to what I believed to be the truth.

Obviously, atheism as a religion was no longer a viable option for me, but what about all of the other different religions in the world? They all disagreed with one another, so they could not all be right. Were any of them right? I wanted to find out.

Now, even though I knew, deep within my being, that God had spoken to me, I didn't turn into a religious fanatic overnight. My experience never really changed my lifestyle or my behavior patterns. The only change in my life at that point was that I was now intensely interested in learning more about God. I am a realist. I am an open-minded person. I didn't start with any agenda to promote any particular religion. I guess you could even say that I was at the time still unconverted, but now I had become extremely curious to learn more about God—whoever He was.

I studied all of the major religions in great detail and many of the more obscure ones, as well, and after four years of intense study I came to the intellectual conclusion that Christianity was the most believable of all the religions that I had examined.

This was actually not an easy conclusion for me come to. Even though I was impressed by the general message of the Bible, particularly the New Testament and the teachings of Jesus, I was thoroughly disillusioned and disappointed with the behavior of most of the people whom I had met throughout my life who had claimed to be Christians. With their mouths, they said they were Christians, but their attitudes, language, and behavior were really no better than my own; and in some cases, I was sure that it was actually worse.

Bad Behavior Produces Defective Disciples

Like many people, I was drawn to Jesus and to Christianity. It was just the people who professed to be Christians whom I did not have much use for, because their behavior did not line up with what came out of their mouths. It bothered me that there was not any sin that you could name and not find someone somewhere claiming to be a Christian who was mixed up in that sin—right up to their eyeballs.

At that point in my life through my job, I was often responsible for training new employees. I would cringe inside whenever someone new would tell me right away that they were a Christian because in the end, it would often turn out that they would be a lousy worker. Some of them proved to be real theological "fruit loops," as well, and their true beliefs often turned out to be far from what the Bible actually teaches.

This proved to be a real stumbling block for me in my own search for salvation. On the one hand, I knew that such behavior testified that they were not right with God. On the other hand, I tended to use their behavior as a balancing scale to justify the continuing sin that was going on in my own life. I deceived myself into thinking that if these sinners were going to make it into heaven, then God wasn't going to keep me out, either. It didn't really occur to me at the time that—according to God's Word—none of us would be going with Jesus when He came for His bride.

I Was Not a Christian; I Only Thought I Was

At that time in my life, I could certainly tell you what the Bible said or did not say. I had read it through numerous times and in several different translations. However, I now understand that knowing *about* God and knowing *what God says* is not the same as trusting God, believing God, and being obedient to Him. It is one thing to acknowledge that God exists, but that is not at all the same thing as being willing to trust and obey Him as our Father in heaven. It is not the same as developing an obedient relationship with God in an intimate and personal way.

Just to give you an idea of how mixed up my concept of Christianity was at that time, let me tell you this one story. In the mid-seventies, I was still a young man in my early twenties, and I was lonely for a female companion. I wasn't looking for hookers or one-night stands. I was looking for a woman to love and to marry and to have as my wife for the rest of my life. I even prayed to God with tears, promising Him that if He brought me a wife, I would serve Him for the rest of my life.

Now, that might seem like a sincere prayer to a lot of people, but after praying such a prayer, I would then go out into the bars and the cabarets and the party houses at night looking for someone who was interested in becoming my wife. One of the more popular bars that I used to frequent was originally called the Devil's Web Cabaret. I realize now how creepy and ironic these actions were, but at the time I didn't see the contradiction between what I was praying for and the way I was living. I was blinded by my own sinful behavior. Later on, I would learn that the Word of God has a lot to say about the way that I was behaving at that point in my life:

> *He that turneth away his ear from hearing the law, even his prayer shall be abomination* (Proverbs 28:9 KJV).

> *God has no use for the prayers of the people who won't listen to him* (Proverbs 28:9 MSG).

A Religious "Conversion" Built upon Deception

The Bible explains to us that one of the greatest obstacles that interferes with people reaching a true salvation experience with God is the fact that our own human nature has been corrupted by evil to such an extent that we can become deceived by our own wickedness. Our own sinfulness will influence us to omit or twist the parts of the Word of God that contradict our evil behavior. We place an overemphasis on any Scriptures that may appear on the surface to excuse or support continuing evil behavior in our lives, but we are blind to the rest of God's Word.

> *The heart is deceitful above all things, and desperately wicked: who can know it?* (Jeremiah 17:9 KJV).

> *There is a way that seems right to a man, but its end is the way of death* (Proverbs 16:25 NKJV).

> *There's a way that looks harmless enough; look again—it leads straight to hell* (Proverbs 16:25 MSG).

That's why it didn't bother me when I met someone at the Devil's Web Cabaret who also professed to be a Christian. We were attracted to one another and eventually made a commitment to love one another. It did not seem wrong to me to move in with someone who already had two children and was separated but still married to someone else, as long as I loved her.

In our own minds, she and I had deceived ourselves into thinking that Christianity was all about philosophical love, and that love trumped everything. I rationalized that because her husband had sinned against his family, he therefore deserved to be rejected, and thus I was justified in taking over where he had failed. From the very beginning, deception was woven into our relationship.

We did not want to be perceived as living in sin, so we lied to our church, to our friends, and to my parents, telling them all that we had eloped and gotten married in another town. Yes, that bothered me, but we felt that we loved one another and it was only a little white lie that would disappear on its own as soon as we could legally get married.

However, it also bothered me when her husband would show up to see his kids and I could see the love in his eyes that he still had for his children. Then it really bothered me when later on he committed suicide. I felt partially responsible, but I rationalized those feelings away with the argument that I really loved this woman and her children. In my mind, the situation was somewhat parallel to what had happened with my own mother and father.

I even went so far as to convince myself that God had taken this man out of the way so that she and I could then get married. The truth is that I was repeating the same sinful path that my own parents had taken. Later on in life, I would learn a hard lesson about what the Word of God means when it says that we reap what we sow in this life.

6

True Christians?

Trying to Be a Christian Without First Submitting to Jesus Christ

My partner and I bought wedding rings to further the charade that we were married, and we went together to the altar at a local church and proclaimed that we believed in Jesus Christ as our Savior. Then we were both baptized shortly afterward in one of the local lakes. We started attending church regularly.

After my partner's husband died in 1976, we were able to actually get married, and a short time later my son was born. We started a successful business and quickly became recognized as pillars of the church and the community. We even sold Bibles and Christian literature through a retail business that we owned. We witnessed to others about God, Jesus, Christianity, and salvation. In our minds, we were just as much Christians as anyone else who said they were a believer. For a short while, it seemed as though we would live happily ever after, but then things started to fall apart.

We made some unwise business decisions that soon left us with a huge load of debt. Our town had been built on the lumber and mining industries, and when they began to falter, suddenly many people were laid off and not spending much money anymore. I could see that our business was headed for bankruptcy, but instead of turning to God, I pulled away from God and away from my wife, returning once again to alcohol and drugs and pornography to deal with the stresses and the emotional instability in my life.

What I did not realize at that time was that turning away from God and back to sin never solves anyone's problems. It only deadens our consciousness of their presence for a short time, but in the process, it actually makes all our problems worse. The more we sin, the more out of touch with reality and the more self-centered we become.

I began to fall into fits of rage and frustration toward my wife and children, just as my own father had done, but the greatest contributor to the destruction of my family was the pornography I began to consume. Contrary to what many believe, pornography is not a marital aid. Yes, it inflames your sexual desire, but it does not inflame your desire for your spouse. Pornography is completely self-centered. Pornography can become so addictive that it increases your desire for sex with anyone, as long as it satisfies your lust. The end result in my own life was that this sexual sin destroyed my marriage.

At first I tried to blame God. Why had God allowed this to happen to me? But Jesus has this to say about the "religion" of those who are unrepentant, no matter what our religion is, Christian or otherwise:

> *What sorrow awaits you.... For you are so careful to clean the outside of the cup and the dish, but inside you are filthy—full of greed and self-indulgence! You blind Pharisees!... You are like whitewashed tombs—beautiful on the outside but filled on the inside with people's bones and all*

sorts of impurity. Outwardly you look like righteous people, but inwardly your hearts are filled with hypocrisy and lawlessness (Matthew 23:25–29 NLT).

My Whole World Collapsed

The Bible tells us that when our houses are built upon the solid rock of the Word of God and the storms of life come, our houses will stand. The truth is that everything but the Word of Jesus Christ is shifting, sinking sand, and when the houses of our lives are built on sinking sand, they may stand for a while, but in the end they will collapse into ruin when trials come.

I had actually managed to survive with one foot standing with Jesus and one foot in a world of unrepentance and continued sinfulness for a long time, but nine years into my life as a professing Christian, the unstable ground on which my success and happiness were built began to shift and shake. Trying to live your life with one foot standing with faith in Christ and one foot involved in continued wickedness simply does not work. Sooner or later, your feet get stretched so far apart that you cannot stop yourself from falling into ruin.

To make matters worse, instead of turning to God to deal with my trials and tribulations, I pulled further away from Him and my wife, moving back into my old sinful ways as everything was collapsing around me.

I had put my trust in my business savvy to provide for my family's future, but by 1981 my businesses were hemorrhaging thousands of dollars every month and we were accumulating a huge amount of debt. It became obvious to me that we were going to lose everything and that there was really nothing I could do to stop it from happening.

The stress of the situation was further increased by the fact that my stepdad had been diagnosed with an aggressive form of cancer and was languishing in a hospital, dying a slow and painful death. My stepfather was far from perfect, but he had raised me and taken care of me from the time I was five years old, and I knew that he loved me as much as he was capable of loving anyone. He was the only dad I had ever really known, and Mom and I were experiencing the stress and trauma of helplessly watching him slowly waste away to less than ninety pounds as a result of the cancer that was devastating his body.

Then, one day in 1981, his suffering was over. The hospital phoned and told us he was gone, and arrangements were made for his funeral to be held the following weekend, but I would never make it to my stepdad's funeral.

It was a Friday night, the night before my stepdad's funeral, when the ground of my own unrepentance and wickedness suddenly gave way underneath me. My wife confronted me with my evildoings toward her and my children, and there was no more denying it. Everything in my life suddenly collapsed. My five-year marriage was all but destroyed. My stepfather was dead. My businesses were in ruins. I was deeply in debt, with no income, and I could even be facing jail time as a result of some of my sinful behavior.

All of my feelings of shame and failure and my sense of condemnation as such a poor husband and father and provider for my family suddenly came to the surface, like a critically open wound, in a single night, and I didn't know where to turn or what to do. It was more than I could handle both spiritually and emotionally, so I got in my car and began to drive. I kept driving for hours, mile after mile, waffling back and forth between the only three options that I could think of.

The devil was working overtime to try to pound it into my

head that I was now at a three-way intersection, a three-way crossroads in my life. I could go back and try to start over; I could keep running and try to start anew; or I could wait for a semi-trailer truck to come in the opposite direction and then swerve my car into its path. I am telling you the truth when I say that the strongest urge by far was the one to simply kill myself and end it all.

7

Believing What God Says

The Three-Way Crossroads

I knew that my life had to change that very night, but I did not know what to do or how to do it, so I continued driving for hundreds of miles as I reviewed the memories of my life and experienced great sorrow over my sins. I was searching for an answer, searching for an escape from the person that I had become. I could turn the car around, go back to my wife, and beg her to give me another chance to start over. Or I could just keep driving, run away from it all, and begin a new life. But finally, I was so ashamed of the way my life had turned out and the things I had done, that I wanted to die. I thought that I deserved to die.

Really, the only thing that stopped me from taking my own life that night was not so much a fear of dying, but the fear of going to hell because of my sins. My parents did not know much about God, but they knew enough to teach me that the wicked go to hell, and my fear of those eternal consequences was just about the only thing that prevented me from giving in to the temptation to take my own life.

The third voice, the voice of hopeless depression and loathing self-condemnation that was fighting the hardest to impose itself upon my mind and my will, was certainly the loudest.

You don't deserve to live. Commit suicide and end it all, it whispered. For six hours, I drove on and on, trying to decide what to do, fighting the urge to commit suicide, praying and crying out to God for an answer as to why this was all happening to me. I didn't realize it at the time, but I know now that Satan was still lying to me. He was still attempting to manipulate me by convincing me that there were only three paths that I could take to get out of this situation, only three directions that I could go. I still did not understand that Satan is a master of the three-way crossroads.

When Satan spoke with Adam and Eve in the Garden of Eden, he enticed them with three specific temptations to get them to embrace evil. He tempted them with pride ("you shall be as gods"). He tempted them with desire ("the forbidden fruit is so pleasing to look at and good for you to eat"). He tempted them with greed ("God has given you permission to enjoy a great abundance of food, all the food that you could ever need, all the food in the Garden, except this fruit from this one tree"). Then Adam and Eve fell from perfection, and death entered our human nature, because they listened to what the devil had to say.

When Satan tempted Jesus in the wilderness at the beginning of His ministry, the devil enticed Jesus with three specific temptations. He encouraged Jesus to tempt God by throwing Himself off the roof of the Temple, because the Word of God had prophesied that God would protect Jesus from harm (the pride of life). After forty days of fasting, Jesus was hungry, so the devil tempted Jesus with the desire for food (the lust of the flesh). Then, finally, he took Jesus up to a high place. He showed Jesus all the kingdoms of the world, promising to give them all to Him if Jesus would only bow down and worship Satan (greed—the lust of the eyes).

Now, here I was in 1981, and Satan was doing exactly the same thing to me. He was doing his best to convince me that I only had three options: I could go back and try to start again, I could run away and try to start afresh, or I could kill myself. Yet none of these answers seemed to be the right answer, the true answer, so I continued to drive my car. As I drove I started pouring my heart out to God, begging for His help, praying for His guidance as to what to do.

We Have More Than Three Choices!

I am telling you that there is more to salvation than just believing in God and experiencing God's presence. There is a very important difference between believing in God and trusting God and believing what He has to say.

In the beginning, the angels of God were created to dwell in the direct presence of God, and yet a third of them fell and will eventually end up in hell. Adam and Eve obviously also believed in God and experienced God's presence because God walked and talked with them, but was that enough to keep them safe from evil? No, it wasn't! Let's take a look first at how Adam and Eve got into trouble in the Garden of Eden.

> *But the Lord God warned him, "You may freely eat the fruit of every tree in the garden—except the tree of the knowledge of good and evil. If you eat its fruit, you are sure to die...."* (Genesis 2:16–17 NLT).

> *"You won't die!" the serpent replied to the woman. "God knows that your eyes will be opened as soon as you eat it, and you will be like God, knowing both good and evil." The woman was convinced. She saw that the tree was beautiful*

> *and its fruit looked delicious, and she wanted the wisdom it would give her. So she took some of the fruit and ate it. Then she gave some to her husband, who was with her, and he ate it, too* (Genesis 3:4–6 NLT).

Here we have the world's first example of two human beings, just like you and me, who believed in God. They believed that God existed and they experienced God's presence, but that was not enough to keep them from dying. It was not enough to keep them out of hell. The real life-and-death questions in this scenario are, "Yes, in the beginning, Adam and Eve believed in God, but did they trust God? Did they believe God's word? Did they obey God?"

The above Scripture passage tells us the answer to these questions. They chose not to trust God. They chose not to believe God's word, and they chose not to obey God, and the consequences of those choices are as follows:

- We all have evil within our natures.
- We all die.
- We are all already condemned to follow Satan into hell if we continue to serve him.

Fortunately for Adam and Eve, and all of the rest of mankind, God could not bear the thought of having all of His children separated from Him and condemned to hell for eternity. Immediately after they sinned, God came to Adam and Eve and had mercy on them, offering them a way of salvation if they wanted to repent and come back into His family.

God declared that man must shed the innocent blood of animals and wear their skins as clothing as a reminder that mankind had brought evil and death into the world. God promised Adam and Eve that He would accept this ritual as a covering for humanity's sin until the time when mankind's Redeemer would be born of one of Eve's descendants. God also declared to Adam and Eve that the promised Redeemer would crush Satan and his dominance over the human race.

The Difference Between Abel and Cain

Adam and Eve originally had the opportunity to choose not to embrace evil. They had the choice to trust God, to believe God, and to obey Him. They could have chosen to reject evil, and the Word of God tells us that—contrary to what Satan wants you to believe—we all still have that same choice today. Satan wants us to believe that because evil became part of our nature when Adam and Eve chose to embrace evil, mankind lost their choice and their ability to reject evil and turn back to God, but this is just another lie of the devil.

Even though the knowledge of evil now resides within every human being, Satan cannot make us sin. He can only influence us toward evil through trials and temptations. He can only lie to try to convince us that we cannot stop sinning. He can only try to deceive us by telling us that we have no other paths to follow than to keep on sinning, but the devil is a liar.

Even after Adam and Eve fell, God gave mankind the opportunity for salvation through repentance and faith in His promise of a Redeemer eventually being born of one of Eve's descendants. The Bible does not specify which creatures were the first to die after evil entered man's domain, but Genesis 3 tells that God Himself made Adam and Eve's first approved clothing out of animal skins, for the shedding of innocent blood was required to cover the inner darkness that had now become part of their beings.

I believe that the Word of God indicates to us that Adam

and Eve did repent, they did turn away from evil, and they tried to teach their children to do the same because the Scriptures reveal that Abel chose to believe God and he turned away from evil. However, Adam and Eve's firstborn son, Cain, rejected God's word. Cain continued to embrace evil. He wanted no part of God's blood sacrifices to cover his sins. Instead, he tried to establish his own form of righteousness based on his own vain works, and eventually his rejection of God's way to salvation turned him into a murderer and destroyed his life.

Jesus said that Satan was a murderer and a liar right from the beginning, and that he is still lying to mankind today. When Satan told Adam and Eve that they would not die if they ate from the tree of knowledge of good and evil, he was effectively trying to murder mankind. When they chose to believe the words of Satan rather than their Father God, he succeeded in bringing death to the entire human race. By convincing Adam and Eve to believe and act on his lies, Satan actually did succeed in murdering Adam and Eve and all of their descendants.

The evolutionists today are trying to convince all of us that death is an evolved process that has always been a part of human life—but that is also a lie. The Bible tells us that God holds Satan responsible for the mortal death of every human who has ever existed. However, God promises us that humanity can take a path that conquers death and leads to eternal life, and Jesus showed us what that path is.

Do You Believe in God?

Listen to me, dear reader! It took me nine years of pain and heartache to learn that believing in God and Jesus Christ is no actual guarantee of salvation. There is a huge awakening going on right now in the realm of Christianity. It is a renewal of faith that emphasizes the belief in the gifts of the Holy Spirit and embracing the presence of God.

I am all for this revival. I think that this renewal of faith in God's Word is a wonderful thing, but I am going to shock some of you by declaring to you that even if we believe in God and proclaim that Jesus is Lord and go to church and sense the presence of God and perform signs and wonders and miracles, it does not necessarily mean that we are on the road to salvation!

The angels of God not only believe that God exists, but they know that God exists, because they were all created to dwell in God's presence in the third heaven. But even though they all knew God existed and they all experienced God's direct presence, one third of them still fell and are now on the path of eternal damnation, eternal separation from God.

God's Word asks, "Do you believe in God? The devils also believe and tremble" (see James 2:19 NKJV). There is more to salvation than just believing in God and experiencing His presence. What about Adam and Eve? They believed in God. They experienced His presence. They walked and talked with God in the Garden of Eden, yet they were still responsible for bringing evil and death to the human race. What about Cain? He believed in God. He talked with God, and God talked with Cain—and look how he ended up.

Only the Starting Point

Do you believe in God and Jesus Christ? That is a good start. It is the first step, but it is not salvation. The Scriptures tell us that if anyone wants to come to God, they must first believe that God exists and is a Rewarder of those who diligently seek Him (see Hebrews 11:6), but there is more to true Christianity than just believing in God and Jesus Christ.

Right now, Christianity is undergoing what many people are referring to as the fifth spiritual Great Awakening. This spiritual awakening is based on a restoration of faith within the Church to believe that the presence, ministry, and gifts of the Holy Spirit are still available to us as Christians today, and they should be pursued as a valuable blessing and an aid to evangelism. This movement also places great emphasis on pursuing and experiencing the presence of God.

Yes, this is all good, but the problem is that many have wrongly supposed that the manifestation of the gifts of the Holy Spirit and the experience of the presence of God is evidence of God's approval on our lives, regardless of how ungodly our actual behavior is. The gifts of the Holy Spirit and the presence of God are treated like some sort of spiritual seal of God's approval, a mystical guarantee that everyone who shares these experiences will all be saved.

Hear me on this! Many professing Christians today are making the exact same mistakes in their lives that I once made myself. The gifts of the Holy Spirit and the presence of God are all good, but they are no guarantee of salvation.

The disciple Judas was directly involved in healing the sick and casting demons out of people for a period of time—but he was not saved. Judas and many of Christ's peers all lived and experienced the direct presence of God in their lives in the person of Jesus Christ, yet the Scriptures tell us that many professing Christians will one day stand before God, only to hear God say, "I do not know you. Depart from Me, you evildoers" (see Luke 13:27 NKJV).

The first step toward salvation is, indeed, to believe that God exists and that He is a Rewarder of those who diligently seek Him. The second step is to seek God out, to desire to dwell in His presence, to desire to talk to God and to have God manifest Himself to us through the Holy Spirit and His gifts, but that still does not bring us to a place of salvation. The Word of God clearly tells us what will bring us to the path of salvation:

> *"Not everyone who says to me, 'Lord, Lord,' will enter the kingdom of heaven, but only the one who does the will of my Father who is in heaven. Many will say to me on that day, 'Lord, Lord, did we not prophesy in your name and in your name drive out demons and in your name perform many miracles?' Then I will tell them plainly, 'I never knew you. Away from me, you evildoers!'"* (Matthew 7:21–23 NIV).

Do You Believe What God Says?

What does it really mean to you when you say that you believe in God and Jesus Christ? Do you believe God's Word when He tells us that not everyone who proclaims that "Jesus is Lord" will enter the Kingdom of heaven? Do you believe Jesus when He tells us that only those who do the will of His Father will enter the Kingdom of heaven? Do you trust and believe Jesus when He tells us that He will reject evildoers even if they have ministered and performed miracles in His name?

In the example of Cain and Abel, both believed in God, both talked with God, but only one man listened to God, only one man trusted God, only one man believed God, only one man obeyed God—and the other did not. God gave Cain the opportunity to change. Did God not talk to Cain personally and give Cain the opportunity to repent and do the right thing?

> *"Why are you so angry?" the Lord asked Cain. "Why do you look so dejected? You will be accepted if you do what is right.*

> *But if you refuse to do what is right, then watch out! Sin is crouching at the door, eager to control you. But you must subdue it and be its master"* (Genesis 4:6–7 NLT).

Cain was lost to Satan because he refused to repent and do the right things. Cain believed in God, but he refused to trust and obey God. Then, if we move ahead to Enoch and Noah's generation, we can see that the presence of God was still available to mankind if they wanted it. God was still personally walking and talking with people in the days of Enoch and Noah.

> *After the birth of Methuselah, Enoch lived in close fellowship with God…walking in close fellowship with God. Then one day he disappeared, because God took him* (Genesis 5:22–24 NLT).

> *This is the account of Noah and his family. Noah was a righteous man, the only blameless person living on earth at the time, and he walked in close fellowship with God.… So God said to Noah…* (Genesis 6:9, 13 NLT).

The opportunity was still available for human beings to walk and talk with God for almost a thousand years after God created Adam and Eve, but by then the entire world was going Cain's way. They believed in God. They believed that God existed, but they were all too busy establishing their own concepts of righteousness. Yet it was not righteousness at all.

God's Word tells us that their thoughts became evil continually. They did not believe God, and they did not obey God anymore. Neither would they believe the words of the prophets that God sent to warn them, and so they all perished in the Flood. All they had to do in order to be saved was to listen to Noah, to repent, and to get aboard the Ark with Noah, and they would have survived; but even though they believed in God, they refused to believe God and obey what God said.

8

Trust and Obey God

Abraham Believed and Obeyed God

Let's move ahead several thousand years, to the life of a man called Abraham. We can see that God is still talking personally today to those who are willing to listen. The book of Romans tells us that what saved Abraham was not that he believed in God, but that he believed what God said and he lived his life accordingly:

> *For what does the Scripture say? Abraham believed God, and it was accounted to him for righteousness* (Romans 4:3 NKJV).

Then, if we move ahead two more generations to Jacob, who is also called Israel, the father and founder of the nation of Israel, we can see that God still talks to mankind. This time, God spoke to Jacob in a dream (see Genesis 28), and Jacob believed God and vowed to serve Him. When we move ahead to when Jacob was 110 years old and as close to dying, we read that he called his son Joseph and gave him this particular blessing for his sons:

> *Then he blessed Joseph and said, "**May the God before whom my grandfather Abraham and my father, Isaac, walked—the God who has been my shepherd all my life, to this very day**, the Angel who has redeemed me from all harm—may he bless these boys. May they preserve my name and the names of Abraham and Isaac. And may their descendants multiply greatly throughout the earth"* (Genesis 48:15–16 NLT, emphasis mine).

So, once again we can see that Abraham and Isaac walked with God and Jacob trusted God as his Shepherd to guide him throughout his life. They all believed what God said, and they obeyed Him.

Moses Trusted and Obeyed God

Next, we move ahead in history a few more generations, to a man named Moses, and we learn that God still spoke directly to people in Moses' day. God spoke to Moses from within the burning bush, and Moses chose to believe God and obey Him. In the end, Moses delivered the entire nation of Israel from the tyranny of Egypt. Trusting and believing God for miracle after miracle, Moses led Israel all the way to the Jordan River, to the very borders of the land that God had promised to the descendants of Abraham.

Furthermore, Moses accomplished this in spite of the fact that over and over, God's people insisted on returning to their own understanding, their own concepts of righteousness, and their old sinful ways.

Finally, when Israel refused to believe God's promise that He would help them defeat the heathen nations in order to claim their inheritance, God decreed that the whole nation would wander in the wilderness until that entire generation of unbelieving adults was dead—except for Joshua and Caleb. They were the only two in the entire nation who had believed what God had said and were willing to act on His promises, and they would be the only ones permitted to enter the Promised Land from that sinful generation:

> *"But even after all he did, you refused to trust the Lord your God, who goes before you looking for the best places to camp, guiding you with a pillar of fire by night and a pillar of cloud by day. When the Lord heard your complaining, he became very angry. So he solemnly swore, 'Not one of you from this wicked generation will live to see the good land I swore to give your ancestors'"* (Deuteronomy 1:32–35 NLT).

Israel Did Not Trust and Obey God

It took forty years of God's miraculous provision in the desert wilderness for that bunch of unbelieving Israelites to die off and the next generation to learn to trust and obey God. Even then, many soon forgot about God. The ranks of the disobedient and unbelieving in Israel rapidly grew again, until God finally withdrew His protection from Israel and the whole nation was taken into slavery by Assyria. Why did this take place? It happened because, even though they believed in God, they continued to sin against God and their fellow man. They stubbornly refused to repent.

> *This disaster came upon the people of Israel* ***because they...sinned against the Lord their God****, who had brought them safely out of Egypt and had rescued them from the power of Pharaoh, the king of Egypt. They had followed the*

practices of the pagan nations the Lord had driven from the land ahead of them, as well as the practices the kings of Israel had introduced. ***The people of Israel had also secretly done many things that were not pleasing to the Lord their God***... *But the Israelites would not listen. They were as stubborn as their ancestors who had refused to believe in the Lord their God. They rejected his decrees and the covenant he had made with their ancestors, and they despised all his warnings*.... *So* ***while these new residents worshiped the Lord, they also worshiped their idols. And to this day their descendants do the same*** (2 Kings 17:7–9, 14–15, 41 NLT, emphasis mine).

Now go and write down these words. Write them in a book. They will stand until the end of time as a witness that ***these people are stubborn rebels who refuse to pay attention to the Lord's instructions****. They tell the seers, "Stop seeing visions!" They tell the prophets, "Don't tell us what is right. Tell us nice things. Tell us lies. Forget all this gloom. Get off your narrow path. Stop telling us about your 'Holy One of Israel.'" This is the reply of the Holy One of Israel: "****Because you despise what I tell you and trust instead in oppression and lies, calamity will come upon you suddenly****—like a bulging wall that bursts and falls. In an instant it will collapse and come crashing down. You will be smashed like a piece of pottery—shattered so completely that there won't be a piece big enough to carry coals from a fireplace or a little water from the well." This is what the Sovereign Lord, the Holy One of Israel, says: "****Only in returning to me and resting in me will you be saved****"* (Isaiah 30:8–15 NLT, emphasis mine).

> *Brothers and sisters, my heart's desire and prayer to God for the Israelites is that they may be saved. For I can testify about them that they are zealous for God, but their zeal is not based on knowledge.* ***Since they did not know the righteousness of God and sought to establish their own, they did not submit to God's righteousness*** (Romans 10:1–3 NIV, emphasis mine).

You have just read God's explanation as to why Israel was still a conquered and occupied nation when Jesus came on the scene. This is why, when John the Baptist and Jesus and the apostles began their ministries in Israel, they all focused on the same basic message: "Repent (turn away from your wickedness) and start trusting and believing God's promises."

This was God's message to Israel, and it is the same message that Jesus and the apostles are preaching to those seeking salvation today. Believe what God has to say about Jesus Christ as mankind's Redeemer and follow Him. Walk as He walked. God's message to Israel—and to every person reading this book today—is to turn away from evil. We must realize that if we were not capable of turning away from evil, then God would not be commanding us to do it.

Once we begin to understand this very basic principle of what God wants us to do in order to come to salvation, it then becomes a matter of whom we are going to choose to believe. Are we going to continue to believe the liar, Satan, who has been ruining our lives up to this point? Are we going to keep sinning, or are we going to turn away from evil to trust in God and Jesus Christ as our Savior?

9

God's Grace Is Not License to Sin

The Dispensation of Grace Will Not Save Us If We Keep Sinning

You may have heard professing Christians declare that since Jesus died for our sins, we are now no longer under the law, but under grace. This is certainly a true statement—if you understand what it means. What it means is that we accept that Jesus Christ has paid the price in full for the sins of all who desire to return to God and accept Jesus as their Savior.

Today we do not condemn people to death for blasphemy, or for stealing, or for lying, or for adultery, or for any other sexual sin, as was the case during Old Testament times. In Canada, we no longer put people to death even for murder—but that does not mean that we should continue to participate in evil behavior. It also does not mean that there will be no consequences for professing Christians who reject God's Word and continue to embrace evil in their behavior.

> *Dear friends, if we deliberately continue sinning after we have received knowledge of the truth, there is no longer any sacrifice that will cover these sins. There is only the terrible expectation of God's judgment and the raging fire that will*

consume his enemies. For anyone who refused to obey the law of Moses was put to death without mercy on the testimony of two or three witnesses. Just think how much worse the punishment will be for those who have trampled on the Son of God, and have treated the blood of the covenant, which made us holy, as if it were common and unholy, and have insulted and disdained the Holy Spirit who brings God's mercy to us (Hebrews 10:26–29 NLT).

There were many people in Israel who opposed Jesus and His teachings because they assumed that their self-righteousness and their religious rituals balanced God's scales enough to make up for any continued evil behavior in their lives, but Jesus refused to accept their false piety and unrepentance.

About this time Jesus was informed that Pilate had murdered some people from Galilee as they were offering sacrifices at the Temple. "Do you think those Galileans were worse sinners than all the other people from Galilee?" Jesus asked. "Is that why they suffered? Not at all! And you will perish, too, unless you repent of your sins and turn to God. And what about the eighteen people who died when the tower in Siloam fell on them? Were they the worst sinners in Jerusalem? No, and I tell you again ***that unless you repent, you will perish, too****"* (Luke 13:1–5 nlt, emphasis mine).

Jesus went through the towns and villages, teaching as he went, always pressing on toward Jerusalem. Someone asked him, "Lord, will only a few be saved?" He replied, "Work hard to enter the narrow door to God's Kingdom, for many will try to enter but will fail. When the master of the house has locked the door, it will be too late. You will stand outside knocking and pleading, 'Lord, open the door for us!' But he will reply, 'I don't know you or where you come from.'

"Then you will say, 'But we ate and drank with you, and you taught in our streets.' And he will reply, 'I tell you, I don't know you or where you come from. Get away from me, all you who do evil.' There will be weeping, and gnashing of teeth, for you will see Abraham, Isaac, Jacob, and all the prophets in the Kingdom of God, but you will be thrown out" (Luke 13:22–28 NLT).

God Commands Us to Stop Sinning!

When Jesus taught that there would be many who would try to enter the narrow door to salvation but would not be able to get through the door, He was explaining to us that no one can get through the door to salvation by performing good works or religious practices. If we reject God's command to repent and turn away from doing evil, we will not be allowed to enter.

When God's Word tells us that Jesus is the Door and the Way to salvation, it refers to more than just realizing and proclaiming that Jesus is God's promised Redeemer of the human race. If we want to be saved, God expects us to repent and follow the example and instructions for salvation that Jesus Christ has provided for us.

Then he said to the crowd, "If any of you wants to be my follower, you must give up your own way, take up your cross daily, and follow me" (Luke 9:23 NLT).

My dear children, I am writing this to you so that you will not sin. But if anyone does sin, we have an advocate who pleads our case before the Father. He is Jesus Christ, the one who is truly righteous. He himself is the sacrifice that atones for our sins—and not only our sins but the sins of all the world. And we can be sure that we know him if we obey his commandments. If someone claims, "I know God," but doesn't obey God's commandments, that person is a liar and is not living in the truth. But those who obey God's word truly show how completely they love him. That is how we know we are living in him. Those who say they live in God should live their lives as Jesus did… And now, dear children, remain in fellowship with Christ so that when he returns, you will be full of courage and not shrink back from him in shame. Since we know that Christ is righteous, we also know that all who do what is right are God's children (1 John 2:1–6, 28–29 NLT).

So why do you keep calling me "Lord, Lord!" when you don't do what I say? I will show you what it's like when someone comes to me, listens to my teaching, and then follows it. It is like a person building a house who digs deep and lays the foundation on solid rock. When the floodwaters rise and break against that house, it stands firm because it is well built. But anyone who hears and doesn't obey is like a person who builds a house right on the ground, without a foundation. When the floods sweep down against that house, it will collapse into a heap of ruins (Luke 6:46–49 NLT).

Jesus Does Not Want Us to Judge and Condemn Others

Most people have heard about the occasion when the religious leaders of Israel caught a woman in the act of adultery and took her into custody. The law of the land at that time stated that adulterers were to be put to death by stoning, so they brought this woman by force before Jesus and threw her at His feet.

These corrupt religious leaders were hoping that Jesus would condemn her to death, and that they could use this to turn the people against Him, but the Word of God tells us that Jesus was not sent to condemn the world but to show us the path to eternal life. The first thing that Jesus did on that day was to deal with the hypocrisy of those who were more than willing to stone this woman to death, even though they all knew that they themselves had sin in their own lives.

> *As he was speaking, the teachers of religious law and the Pharisees brought a woman who had been caught in the act of adultery. They put her in front of the crowd. "Teacher," they said to Jesus, "this woman was caught in the act of adultery. The law of Moses says to stone her. What do you say?" They were trying to trap him into saying something they could use against him, but Jesus stooped down and wrote in the dust with his finger. They kept demanding an answer, so he stood up again and said, "All right, but let the one who has never sinned throw the first stone!" Then he stooped down again and wrote in the dust. When the accusers heard this, they slipped away one by one, beginning with the oldest, until only Jesus was left in the middle of the crowd with the woman* (John 8:3–9 NLT).

We Are Condemned Already

There is much more to be learned from the story of the

adulterous woman than just the fact that Jesus spared her from being stoned to death. Many unlearned people have the wrong idea about Christianity and Jesus Christ. They think that God sends people to hell just because they reject Jesus. That is a terrible distortion of the truth that God wants us to understand about heaven and hell.

Rejecting Jesus doesn't send people to hell. God's Word tells us that the entire human race is already condemned to be eternally separated from God—because we are all sinners who, each one of us, have chosen to embrace evil to certain degrees in our lives. God's purpose in sending Jesus Christ to earth for us was to send Someone who had the power and the authority and the desire to save and redeem us from the state of condemnation in which the whole world already exists.

The truth is that we all have sin on our life's record. Every single one of the adulterous woman's accusers were under the exact same condemnation that she was. In God's eyes, they were all worthy of death. Each of them had sin in their lives. Once they realized that their hypocrisy had been exposed, her accusers' consciences shamed them, and they all retreated from the Son of God and returned to the darkness from which they had come.

> *For God so loved the world that he gave his one and only Son, that whoever believes in him shall not perish but have eternal life. For God did not send his Son into the world to condemn the world, but to save the world through him. Whoever believes in him is not condemned, but whoever does not believe stands condemned already because they have not believed in the name of God's one and only Son. This is the verdict: Light has come into the world, but people loved*

darkness instead of light because their deeds were evil. Everyone who does evil hates the light, and will not come into the light for fear that their deeds will be exposed. But whoever lives by the truth comes into the light, so that it may be seen plainly that what they have done has been done in the sight of God (John 3:16–21 NIV).

10

Already Condemned

We Are All Like the Adulterous Woman

When it comes to guilt, God's Word declares that we are all guilty and worthy of death, but we can all learn a great deal from the story of this adulterous woman. First, her sin had resulted in her being taken into captivity. She was no longer free. Second, her sin had placed her under the sentence of death and there was no escape for her. If Jesus had not been present to intercede for her, the woman would most certainly have been put to death that very day.

Another important thing to note is that the woman did not even willingly come to Jesus on her own. I am sure that she was terrified, as her accusers forcibly tossed her at the feet of Jesus as if she were a piece of human garbage to be disposed of, but they had not counted on the fact that Jesus loved her.

Even though she was a sinner, the truth is that Jesus was willing to set her free and even to die for this woman's salvation—while she was still a sinner.

> *When we were utterly helpless, Christ came at just the right time and died for us sinners. Now, most people would not be willing to die for an upright person, though someone might perhaps be willing to die for a person who is especially good.*

> *But God showed his great love for us by sending Christ to die for us while we were still sinners. And since we have been made right in God's sight by the blood of Christ, he will certainly save us from God's condemnation. For since our friendship with God was restored by the death of his Son while we were still his enemies, we will certainly be saved through the life of his Son. So now we can rejoice in our wonderful new relationship with God because our Lord Jesus Christ has made us friends of God* (Romans 5:6–11 NLT).

One of the primary lessons to be learned from the story of Christ's encounter with the adulterous woman in this passage is that even while we are still condemned sinners and not even looking for God, Jesus still loves us. He still forgives us. He does not want to judge us. At the time when Christ met her, this woman was not looking for Jesus nor was she seeking spiritual salvation. She was brought forcibly before Jesus and dumped at His feet by her accusers.

There was no question that the adulterous woman was guilty of committing the sins she was accused of, but Jesus did not condemn her. He showed her mercy and forgiveness. He set her free from her death sentence, but Jesus did not even stop there. He gave her a very specific command to go and sin no more—and He gave her the spiritual strength to do just that.

Free to Stop Sinning

This is actually the main point of the message that God is trying to convey to us in this story in His Word. I was once like many professing Christians today, who continue to stumble around in habitual sinful behavior because they do not understand that they can be set free from the chains of sin that have held them captive for all of their lives. Through the story of the adulterous woman, Jesus showed this woman—and all of us—an open door of escape, and He has commanded us to go through it and receive salvation.

Jesus was not giving mankind advice in this passage. He was not showing us an optional avenue of behavior that we could choose to either follow or ignore. No, Jesus sets us free from our condemnation and our death sentence, but then He commands us to go and sin no more. Jesus would not require us to do this without empowering us through the Holy Spirit to be able to obey His instruction.

> *So now there is no condemnation for those who belong to Christ Jesus. And because you belong to him, the power of the life-giving Spirit has freed you from the power of sin that leads to death.... God did what the law could not do. He sent his own Son in a body like the bodies we sinners have. And in that body God declared an end to sin's control over us by giving his Son as a sacrifice for our sins. He did this so that the just requirement of the law would be fully satisfied for us, who no longer follow our sinful nature but instead follow the Spirit.*
>
> *Those who are dominated by the sinful nature think about sinful things, but those who are controlled by the Holy Spirit think about things that please the Spirit. So letting your sinful nature control your mind leads to death. But letting the Spirit control your mind leads to life and peace... Therefore, dear brothers and sisters, you have no obligation to do what your sinful nature urges you to do. For if you live by its dictates, you will die. But if through the power of the Spirit you put to death the deeds of your sinful*

nature, you will live. For all who are led by the Spirit of God are children of God (Romans 8:1–6, 12–14 NLT).

Are you hearing what the Spirit of God is saying to you here? If you claim to be a Christian, then you need to believe God's promise that the power of Christ's life-giving Spirit has freed you from the power of sin that leads to death. Through Christ, God has declared that sin no longer has control over those who refuse to follow their sinful nature, but allow themselves to be controlled by the Holy Spirit. Thus you no longer have any obligation to do what your sinful nature urges you to do.

No Condemnation for Followers of Christ

This is a perfectly accurate statement, if we truly understand what it means. Unfortunately this is a Scripture passage that is often twisted and wrongly used by many who claim to be Christians yet who are continuing to allow their sinful natures to control their minds, their speech, and their behavior.

I implore you to listen to the truth about this. We are not going to get away with taking parts of the Word of God out of context and ignoring the parts that say that if we continue to live by the dictates of our sinful nature, we will surely die.

Let's use the adulterous woman as an example. Jesus loved her. He did not condemn her. He showed mercy and compassion toward her. He forgave her, delivered her from her death sentence, and set her free. Then He told her to go and sin no more.

Now think carefully about this: What do you suppose would have happened if this woman had then chosen to ignore the instruction of Jesus to "go and sin no more"? The truth is that if the woman had refused to obey Jesus and instead returned to her old sinful ways, she would have put herself back under the condemnation of the law, and the next time that she was caught in the act of adultery, she would surely have been put to death as a transgressor. When we are repentant, Christ sets us free from the law of sin and death; but when we are unrepentant, we put ourselves back under the law of sin and death. The Word of God tells us that the law and those who administer the law are supposed to exist in order to be a terror to those who are determined to do evil.

11

God Still Speaks

Repentance Opens the Door

Jesus is the only Door to eternal life, but God's message to mankind—from Genesis to Revelation—has never changed. It has always been "repent and believe God's promise of a Redeemer." Yes, Jesus is the only Door to our salvation, but repentance (that is, turning away from evil) is what moves us from darkness to light in order to be able to see the Door. Repentance is what brings us to the Door, and repentance is what God requires of us if we want to enter through the Door that leads to salvation.

Every book in the Old Testament and every prophet from Abel to John the Baptist remind humanity that we all need to repent and believe in God's promise of the coming Redeemer. Then Jesus came along preaching, "Repent. I am the Redeemer. I am the Messiah." Then the apostles came along preaching, "Repent. Jesus is not only the Redeemer and Messiah of Israel, but He is also the Savior of the entire world."

It is astounding to me that there are so many professing Christians today who have no trouble hearing the part of God's message that says that Jesus is our Savior, yet they are totally deaf to the first part of God's message commanding us to repent and turn away from our sins. Yes, Jesus is the only Door to our salvation, but repentance is the only way to open the Door and pass through to that salvation. After that, Jesus shows us the way to walk. Following Jesus in repentant obedience is the only way we can stay on the narrow path that leads to salvation and eternal life in God's Kingdom.

God's Word Applies to Me Personally

Even though I had called myself a Christian before that day in 1981, I had been trying to live my life through vain confidence in myself, according to my own warped sense of self-righteousness. It was not until I hit rock bottom in my life that I understood that this kind of Christianity simply does not work. It is not true Christianity. It is a false way that does not lead to salvation.

Have you ever heard someone say that they "tried" Christianity and it didn't work for them? That's because they tried a false Christianity, one that didn't include true repentance, that is, turning away from evil and totally putting their complete faith and trust in God. Until we set our sights on loving God with all our heart, our soul, and our mind, we are still following Satan. Until we choose to follow Jesus in obedience to all of His commands, we are still in bondage to Satan and the laws of sin and death.

I now realize that on that day in 1981, God had allowed me to get to such a low place in my life in order to be truly set free. I finally reached the place where I had to admit that it was not God's fault that my life was a shambles. It was my own fault because I had not fully trusted God. I had not believed God. I had not been fully obedient to God. I had tried to serve God and yet still keep some of my own sins. I thought that I was independent and free, but at last I came to the place where I realized that I was still a prisoner to sin and to Satan. It simply does not work to try to have one foot in the Kingdom of God and one foot still in unrepentance and ungodliness.

> *So the Lord must wait for you to come to him so he can show you his love and compassion. For the Lord is a faithful God. Blessed are those who wait for his help. O people of Zion, who live in Jerusalem, you will weep no more. He will be gracious if you ask for help. He will surely respond to the sound of your cries* (Isaiah 30:18–19 NLT).

> *I prayed to the Lord, and he answered me. He freed me from all my fears.... In my desperation I prayed, and the Lord listened; he saved me from all my troubles.... Come, my children, and listen to me.... Does anyone want to live a life that is long and prosperous? Then keep your tongue from speaking evil and your lips from telling lies! Turn away from evil and do good. Search for peace, and work to maintain it. The eyes of the Lord watch over those who do right; his ears are open to their cries for help. But the Lord turns his face against those who do evil; he will erase their memory from the earth. The Lord hears his people when they call to him for help. He rescues them from all their troubles. The Lord is close to the brokenhearted; he rescues those whose spirits are crushed.... Calamity will surely destroy the wicked, and those who hate the righteous will be punished. But the Lord will redeem those who serve him. No one who takes refuge in him will be condemned* (Psalm 34:4–22 NLT).

The Path of Repentance and Obedience

Ever since God spoke to Adam and Eve in the Garden of

Eden, the door of repentance and the path of choosing to return to a life of trusting and obeying God has always been available to mankind, but I never understood this for the first twenty-eight years of my life. I was blinded by Satan's deception. I did not comprehend or believe that I could stop sinning, and I did not really grasp that God required me to stop sinning.

On that day in 1981, I finally understood that this was the answer for which I had been searching. It was the piece of the puzzle that had always been missing from my religion and my life. The Bible explains in simple language where Adam and Eve went wrong—and why my own life was lying in ruins at that moment in time. I had made the same mistake that Adam and Eve had made. I had not trusted in the Lord with all my heart. I had not shunned all evil in my life. I had not fully submitted to God in every area. I had been trying to build my life through leaning on my own wisdom and my own perceptions of good works and righteousness—and eventually everything that I had built had ultimately collapsed into rubble.

In 1972, I had come to the realization that God existed. God had spoken to me, Spirit to spirit, at that time, declaring that He had spared my life. I believed that Jesus was the Savior of the world. Without proper Christian teaching and guidance, I mistakenly thought that this meant that everything was okay between myself and God back then, but I didn't really trust God yet and I didn't believe everything that God had to say. I was still a slave to Satan.

I had been listening to the devil's arguments that I was incapable of being set free of all of my sins and addictions. I listened to his lies, telling me that continued wickedness in parts of my life would not destroy me. "You will not die!" the devil promised. Yet my sin did destroy my life, and listening to Satan almost drove me to suicide. It was only when God allowed me to come to that crossroads in 1981 that I truly understood what the book of Matthew was talking about when it said:

> *Because strait is the gate, and narrow is the way, which leadeth unto life, and few there be that find it* (Matthew 7:14 KJV).

This is not some new teaching. Right after Adam and Eve made their original choice to sin, God had mercy on them. Mankind would still have to experience mortal death because of the evil that now resided in the nature of human beings, but God also gave man an offer of redemption from the hell of eternal subservience to Satan.

God encouraged Adam and Eve to repent (that is, to turn away from evil and turn back to God), promising that one of Eve's descendants would become the Redeemer for the entire human race. God promised that all who put their faith in Him would be saved and adopted back into His family, but God also expects us to demonstrate our faith through trust and obedience.

God Expects Us to Repent

I have learned that it is very important to listen carefully to the Word of God and obey what He tells us to do. How we respond to God today can affect our lives for many years to come.

There can be no denying that the marital relationship between myself and my wife started out in an ungodly manner, a sinful way, but God is a forgiving God. We started off badly, but there is no doubt in my mind whatsoever that if I had truly understood God's way to salvation back then, repented of my wicked ways, and then taught my family to do the same and follow Jesus Christ, God would have forgiven us and blessed our family. I believe that this is true for every person reading this book, as well. Is your life now a mess because of your past behavior? Repent now. It's not too late. God can still forgive you and help you to start over.

How do I know this to be true? I know it because there is not any sin in existence that God is not willing to forgive if we turn away from evil and back to God again. God forgave Adam and Eve for bringing evil into the world in the first place. Even after such a terrible transgression, God still offered them a path to salvation.

Consider King David, as well. The Bible tells us of King David spying on Bathsheba while she was bathing, naked, and David became so inflamed by his lust for her that he sent her husband into battle and ordered his soldiers to abandon him to the enemy so that he would be slain. David literally committed murder so that he could commit adultery—and God still forgave him when he sincerely repented and turned back to the Lord again.

> *I have found David the son of Jesse, a man after mine own heart, which shall fulfil all my will* (Acts 13:22 KJV).

That does not mean that there would not be long-lasting consequences both during and after David's lifetime for his sins, but God still forgave David. If you want to know what it was about Jesse's son David that caused God to honor him as a man after God's own heart, in spite of David's failures, you'll find the answer in the Psalms written by David. In them we find that, even though David sinned grievously in his life, he eventually learned to trust and obey God:

- Psalm 31:14 KJV: But I trusted in thee, O Lord.
- Psalm 34:22 NIV: No one who takes refuge in him will be condemned.
- Psalm 118:8 KJV: It is better to trust in the Lord than to put confidence in man.

This is where I was also misled by my own vanity and my own sinful heart as a young man. Even though I had acknowledged God's existence and accepted that Jesus was the Savior of humanity, I had not learned to trust, believe, and obey what God says to us. Whenever a conflict arose between the Word of God and what I wanted to think, say, or do, I placed my confidence in my own abilities and wisdom. I chose to follow a sinful path, and yet I was still convinced that this would bring me love, joy, peace, success, and fulfilment in my life. In the end, it was my twisted confidence in myself—rather than in God—that destroyed both me and my family.

Searching for God in All the Wrong Places

During the 1970s, I had become aware of God's presence and was endeavoring to learn about God. The problem was, I had not grasped that knowing about God and knowing what God has to say is not the same as determining to develop a personal relationship with God through repentance, trust, faith, and obedience.

Spiritual blindness is a strange thing. At the time, I simply could not see the truth, and I had no one to teach me as I am now teaching others. I understand now that it is possible to have tons of Scripture memorized and go to church to sing and pray and practice all kinds of religious rituals and traditions, but still end up far from God.

If we refuse to walk in obedience and apply God's Word to our personal lives, we are deceiving ourselves. Those who try to justify continuing wickedness in their own lives, by comparing their lives to the lives of other people, are not really praying to God when they pray. They are actually praying to themselves, trying to justify their own sins by praying to a God of their own making.

> *"Two men went to the Temple to pray. One was a Pharisee, and the other was a despised tax collector. The Pharisee stood by himself and prayed this prayer: 'I thank you, God, that I am not a sinner like other people—cheaters, sinners, adulterers. I'm certainly not like that tax collector! I fast twice a week, and I give you a tenth of my income.' But the tax collector stood at a distance and dared not even lift his eyes to heaven as he prayed. Instead, he beat his chest in sorrow, saying, 'O God, be merciful to me, for I am a sinner.' I tell you, this sinner, not the Pharisee, returned home justified before God* (Luke 18:10–14 NLT).

At the Feet of Jesus

When I was driving along the highway that fateful day in 1981, all of my blindness and false pride was stripped away from me. I knew that I was a sinner deserving of death. Satan was doing his best to pressure me to take my own life, but I did not really want to die. I wanted to live! I did not want to continue serving Satan in hell for the rest of eternity. I wanted to be with God. I wanted to overcome evil in my life, so that I could live for God and be obedient to Him, but I did not know how to do it.

The weight of my sin and guilt was so heavy upon me that I

felt as if I were being crushed emotionally and spiritually to the point of death. I could hardly breathe. With all that was in me, I started crying out to God to be merciful to me, to lift this burden from my heart, and to help me to change.

All of a sudden, I became so overwhelmed by the sense of God's presence and His love for me, that I began to weep uncontrollably. This was not normal crying. It was agonizing, soul-wrenching groans that came from the deepest recesses of my being. It was so intense that I could barely see to drive, so I pulled into the small town of Williams Lake, looking for someplace to park until I could function normally again.

It was early Saturday morning by then, and the town was all but deserted, so I just picked a random parking space along the main street. I pulled into it and bowed my head against the steering wheel for a long time, praying and crying until at last I regained my composure. I am not sure how long I remained bowed over the steering wheel experiencing wave after wave of God's love, mercy, and forgiveness, but eventually it began to fade—until then, for the second time in my life, I had the assurance that God was speaking to me and this is what I heard:

> You are at a crossroads in your life, but it is not the three-way crossroads that the devil has presented to you. There is a fourth path, and it is the only path that leads to eternal life. The reason that you are in your present situation is that you have never truly repented. You have never fully turned away from evil and chosen to trust and follow Me. Now evil wants to totally destroy you. If you commit suicide tonight, you will die lost and be forever subjugated to the father whom you have been serving.

Neither will it profit you to go back and start over, or keep running away. At this crossroads in your life, all paths that do not lead directly to Me are actually leading you further away from Me. If you keep following them, they will all eventually lead to destruction and the same destination in the end.

The choices that you have been considering may seem to be three different paths, but wide is the road and broad is the way that leads to destruction, and straight is the gate and narrow is the path that leads to eternal life. In the end, all paths except one lead to the same destination—eternal servitude to the evil father whom you have chosen to believe.

Without repentance, desire, greed, and pride will always bring mankind to the same destination of eternal separation from God, and they will forge many chains of bondage and torment along the way. Yet there has always been a fourth path for man to take: the path that Jesus took. It is the only one that will truly change your life and set you free. You need to truly repent and follow Jesus.

Finally, I understood what God was saying to me. There is no other way for any of us to be saved aside from fully turning away from evil. We must respond in faith to God's promise of a Redeemer and choose to fully follow Jesus Christ in total obedience.

It's not that we will never stumble during our journey back to God. We will still sometimes make mistakes in the things that we think and say and do. We will all fail at times. God knows that. God knows that none of us is perfect, but God requires that we have a truly repentant heart and endeavor to do the best we can to listen to the daily guidance of the Holy Spirit, who enables us to follow and obey Jesus Christ in our journey back to the Father God.

The truth is that we are all only spiritual children learning to walk with Jesus. When we do stumble along the way, Jesus still loves us. His hand will always be there to help us stand up again, but habitual sinners will not get away with their wickedness forever. Eventually, those who are unrepentant will pay a heavy price for their continued evildoings.

12

Knock, Knock! Who's There?

Is It Okay for Christians to Keep Sinning?

As a minister, I sometimes run into opposition from people who think they can keep on sinning and still go to heaven. They believe this, because they have not been properly taught about the subjects of repentance and obedience. When you talk to them about God's requirement for us to repent and be obedient, they will often quote Scriptures that declare that we are saved by grace through faith in Jesus Christ and not by our own works.

These people have been taught a "false gospel," and as a result, they fail to understand that "repentance" and "obedience" are not the same things as "works." They are different concepts altogether. Repentance and obedience are products of a right attitude toward God. We cannot earn salvation through our repentance and obedience any more than we can earn salvation by performing good works, but repentance and obedience are evidence that our hearts are right before God.

Another opposition that happens when you bring up God's requirement for us to repent and remain repentant in order to be saved is the argument that "we are no longer under the law." Again, God's Word explains that "repentance" and the "law" are two different things.

God's requirement for us to repent and believe in His

promised Redeemer has existed ever since the Garden of Eden. Repentance is the call of God's Spirit to turn away from evil, to love God, and to love our fellow man. Jesus said that we are doing well if we do these things. All of the rest of the "law" was introduced during the time of Moses because of humanity's rebellion and refusal to repent without legislation.

Unrepentance in the Church

In the book of Revelation, Jesus Christ Himself takes almost three whole chapters to address problems that were already beginning to surface in corporate Christianity during the first century of its conception. The book of Revelation was written by the apostle John when he was in exile on the Isle of Patmos near the end of his life's ministry.

There are some leaders who have made efforts to suggest that the seven churches in the first chapters of the book of Revelation represent different denominations. Others teach that the seven churches refer to different stages of the Church in history, with the lukewarm church of Laodicea being the predominant state of Christianity in the last days before Christ's return.

Yes, there are perhaps some elements of truth to these observations, but we must be careful not to miss the more important teaching that Jesus repeats seven times throughout chapters 2 and 3 of the book of Revelation:

> *Whoever has ears, let them hear what the Spirit says to the churches* (Revelation 3:22 NIV).

Even though Jesus addresses each church individually, He finishes each package of warnings and exhortations with the same phrase, addressing all the churches. Why? Jesus did this because each of the positive and negative aspects that Jesus was referring to can exist in any church. Jesus was encouraging all of us to continue walking in the Spirit, but He was also warning us to deal with the unrepentance that exists within our lives.

> *Those whom I love I rebuke and discipline. So be earnest and repent. Here I am! I stand at the door and knock. If anyone hears my voice and opens the door, I will come in and eat with that person, and they with me. To the one who is victorious, I will give the right to sit with me on my throne, just as I was victorious and sat down with my Father on his throne* (Revelation 3:19–21 NIV).

Many preachers like to paint the picture of Jesus standing at the door of the unbeliever's heart knocking, but that is only a half truth. Here, in the book of Revelation, Jesus is addressing unrepentant, professing Christians in the same way that He was trying to reach unrepentant, sinful Israel. He is addressing the churches and telling us that He is standing at the door of our hearts, politely knocking to be let in.

We Are the First Door

Many people have not been properly taught that there are two doors on the path of salvation. The first is the door of our heart. Regardless of our profession about being a Christian, if we are unrepentant, our door is turned toward darkness, and Jesus and the Holy Spirit are left on the outside, knocking in order to be allowed back in. When we choose to believe God and repent, our hearts are turned toward God's light so Jesus and the Holy Spirit can enter in. Then we have the inner light and the spiritual power necessary to enable us to see the path to salvation and take up our cross to follow Jesus along that path.

Professing Christians love the image of Jesus knocking at the door of the unbeliever's heart and asking to be let in, but this message from Jesus in the book of Revelation is not a message to the heathen. This message is to the churches. We must hear what the Spirit is saying to every one of the churches in Revelation 3:20: "Behold, I stand at the door, and knock; if any man hear my voice, and open the door, I will come in to him, and will sup with him, and he with me" (KJV).

Today, Jesus is standing, knocking at the door of the hearts of professing, backslidden Christians. All throughout Christianity, Jesus is knocking on people's hearts, wanting to come in. Preachers do not do professing Christians any favors by suggesting that they are not sinners, only forgetful and thus not responsible for their continued disobedience.

Our hearts are doors that can only face one way. When we turn our hearts away from God and toward sinfulness and darkness, we leave Jesus and the Holy Spirit on the outside, continually knocking on the backs of our doors to be allowed back in. Jesus Christ will not force Himself into our lives. Whether or not He will come in and abide with us is totally dependent upon which way the doors to our hearts are facing.

When Adam and Eve turned away from God in rebellion and disobedience, the doors of their hearts were turned toward evil and darkness, leaving God on the outside, knocking to be allowed back in. Then, when they turned their hearts toward God, choosing to repent and believe in God's promise of a Redeemer, light came back into their lives because their doors were once again facing the Lord, and God was able to enter in and fellowship with them once again.

The way to salvation today is exactly the same as it was six thousand years ago. It is only when we turn back to God's light and repent that Jesus is able to come into our hearts again, and the Holy Spirit is able to heal us and help us to get up and continue on the narrow path of repentance, following Jesus in faith and obedience to our Father God.

In the book of Matthew, it is only the repentant—the five wise virgins—who will have the abiding light of Jesus and the Holy Spirit within them to be able to find the second door, the door of heaven that will open for us when the Bridegroom comes. Then that door will be closed, and the unrepentant will be left behind to share the fate of the heathen—and Christ's response to the unrepentant professing Christians will be, "Depart from Me, evildoers, workers of iniquity. I do not know you" (see Luke 13:27).

Salvation will still be available for all who are left on earth at that time, but the door to heaven for the living will remain closed for seven more years, and no one will be spared the horrors of the seven-year Tribulation as a consequence of their continued unrepentance and disobedience. God does not want that to happen to any of us.

It took me many years to learn that when we hear the message of the Gospel and turn to God in repentance and faith in Jesus Christ, the doors of our hearts are facing God. We are facing the grace and mercy and forgiveness of God. The light of God pushes out the darkness in our lives, and Jesus can enter in and dwell with us. As long as we determine to continue to face God and make progress toward Him on the narrow path of repentance and obedience, Jesus and the Holy Spirit will always be with us to guide and help us on to victory.

Jesus Is the Second Door— The Only Way to Salvation

The second Door that the Bible tells us is necessary for our salvation is Jesus Himself. God wants us to understand that Jesus is the only Door that provides entry for the human race to be restored to God's family.

> *Then said Jesus unto them again, Verily, verily, I say unto you, I am the door of the sheep. All that ever came before me are thieves and robbers: but the sheep did not hear them. I am the door: by me if any man enter in, he shall be saved, and shall go in and out, and find pasture* (John 10:7–9 KJV).

Jesus is the Light that shines in the darkness, but it is the turning of our heart's doors away from darkness toward the Light (repentance) that enables us to see God's Door. It is also the key to unlocking the doorway to eternal life. We cannot come into God's Kingdom through Jesus if we insist on continuing to walk in sin and darkness, in the opposite direction to the one that Jesus walks. The only way out of the darkness is to turn toward the Light of God and follow Him.

> *Jesus spoke to the people once more and said, "I am the light of the world. If you follow me, you won't have to walk in darkness, because you will have the light that leads to life"* (John 8:12 NLT).

> *"Don't let your hearts be troubled. Trust in God, and trust also in me...." Jesus told him, "I am the way, the truth, and*

the life. No one can come to the Father except through me" (John 14:1, 6 NLT).

"I have come as a light to shine in this dark world, so that all who put their trust in me will no longer remain in the dark. I will not judge those who hear me but don't obey me, for I have come to save the world and not to judge it" (John 12:46–47 NLT).

My Chains Are Gone—I've Been Set Free!

In the old hymn "Amazing Grace," there is a verse that begins with the words, "My chains are gone, I've been set free." On that day in 1981, as I turned to God in complete repentance, it was like a blindfold of darkness had been ripped away from my eyes and I could finally see the truth. For the first time in my life, I suddenly understood what the writer of that song meant with those words.

Just because we have the knowledge of evil within our nature, this does not mean that we have to sin. The truth is that Satan cannot make us sin if we really want to overcome sin and follow Jesus. Satan only offered Adam and Eve three choices. He only offered Jesus three choices. All he ever offers any of us is three choices. He entices us to sin through the pride of life (vanity). He tempts us to sin through lust of the eyes (desire), and he urges us to sin through the lust of the flesh (greed)—but listen to me: There is another path available for us!

God showed me that there is a fourth path for us to follow in life—the path of repentance, the path of trusting in God's Word and walking with Jesus in obedience to God. If we choose to follow Jesus, God promises us that Satan cannot force us to continue sinning. God will enable us through the Holy Spirit to do what He is asking us to do: to overcome and to be victorious over sin.

> *Trust in the Lord with all your heart; do not depend on your own understanding. Seek his will in all you do, and he will show you which path to take* (Proverbs 3:5–6 NLT).

God Showed Me the Path

If you doubt that God will be there to show you which path to take, let me share with you what happened right after I made the commitment to fully repent and obey God with all my heart. When I lifted my head up from the steering wheel, at around nine in the morning, I really had no idea where I was. I had parked in some random downtown street parking space because I was an emotional basket case and couldn't see any more to drive.

I had never been to downtown Williams Lake before. I had only driven through the outskirts of the town on my way to somewhere else. Yet when I lifted my head off the steering wheel and looked at the building right in front of me, I could see that it was a lawyer's office—and there was someone inside.

I already knew that if I was going to fully repent and follow God, I would have to return to my hometown. I would need to face the consequences of my past sins and try as much as possible to make things right with my wife and children. I knew that this was going to require getting psychological counseling and acquiring legal advice, especially with the consideration of potential jail time for some of the things that I had done, but I was ready to put God's Word to the test.

I got out of the car and tried to open the door of the lawyer's office, but it was locked, so I knocked on the door until the man inside answered. When he came to the door, all of my emotions just flooded out again onto this poor fellow as I told him my story, complete with my commitment that I wanted to make God the Lord of my life. Well, surprise, surprise! It turned out that this lawyer was a Christian, a real Christian lawyer, a man who understood that this was a divine appointment from God.

He wasn't open on Saturdays. What lawyer is? He had just felt that it was important for him to go in to the office to catch up on some work—and then I showed up. I don't even remember the man's name. I just remember that he prayed with me. He encouraged me and told me that I was doing the right thing. He gave me some good legal advice. He recommended a psychologist and a lawyer located closer to where I lived.

Then I headed back to my hometown to begin my new life, determined that I was going believe what God said rather than Satan. Sure, I've stumbled on occasion and I have had to repent and ask God for forgiveness. We all do—but ever since that day, I have tried my best to trust in God rather than in my own understanding. I have done my best to walk with God in repentance and obedience, rather than in the ways that had ruined my life.

The Word of God says that when we get to this place in our lives, we become born again. We actually become a new creature through Jesus Christ, and I don't doubt that at all. I have never for one moment ever regretted my decision that day to turn away from evil and truly follow Jesus Christ.

Some years later, when I ran into an old buddy from my sinful days and I was sharing with him how God had changed my life, he made the comment that if the person who I was back then ran into the person who I am now, we wouldn't get along at all—and he was right! I am a completely different person today.

I am no longer the person who used to throw empty liquor bottles into the parking lots of churches, calling the people who went there hypocrites. I am no longer the man who used to tear past churches, revving my motorcycle while church was in session just to annoy the people inside.

More importantly, I am no longer the person whose life was ruled by and imprisoned by sin and addictions, yet thinking that he was just as good as so many professing Christians and even better than some. Now I am the person who is teaching the way to salvation to people both inside the Church and outside of the Church. Today I do my best to lead others to Christ while keeping my own sinful desires subject to the Lord, conscious of the fact that I myself do not want to end up a castaway after having led others to Jesus.

Don't Expect God to Always Fix Our Mess Ups

Over the past thirty-five years since I turned my life over to Jesus, I have seen God do some miraculous things in my own life and in the lives of many other people. Yet God doesn't always make everything go away or return them to the way they were before we destroyed them all, just because we become Christians, particularly when it involves past sins that we have committed.

On the contrary, there are very real consequences for those who follow evil for a time. Yes, God will always forgive us if we return to Him with a truly repentant heart, but the consequences of a single sinful indiscretion in our lives can continue to have serious repercussions on earth for generations to come.

Adam and Eve turned back to God, but we still all die because of their original sin. Their firstborn son still murdered his brother as a result of the sin nature that Adam and Eve brought into the human race. Both Noah and Lot had problems with drunkenness that brought shame and conflict into their families.

Abraham, Jacob, David, and Solomon all ignored God's instructions not to have more than one wife, and the offspring from each of their indiscretions grew up to become enemies of Israel. In fact, their Arab descendants are still enemies of Israel to this very day.

David repented of his sin of murder, but Absalom, a son of David's by one of his extra wives, also became a murderer, and in the end he tried to murder his own father, David, and take over the throne. Then there was the thief on the cross. Jesus forgave him, but the thief still had to suffer and die on the cross that day for the sins that he had committed.

Don't think that becoming a Christian means that the results of all of our past sins will magically vanish and that there will be no consequences for any sins that we have committed in the past, or that we commit now or in the future. Any person who has a television knows that there are numerous prominent Christians and Christian ministers throughout the world today whose families, ministries, and reputations have all been ruined because of continuing unrepentant sin in their lives.

Continuing sin always has consequences. If you think that you are immune from such consequences, you are only deceiving yourself. I attended Bible college from 1985 to 1987, and many of the students who also attended there have seen their lives seriously damaged as a result of unrepentant sin. Some have even died. Even the school itself eventually withered and died as a result of the administration being more concerned about pleasing man rather than pleasing God.

Did God fix everything that I had messed up during my years of disobedience? No! God helped me restore some things—but not everything. I have learned that some bad things that we have done in life cannot be undone despite our best efforts to make them right. All we can do is try to do our best to move on and not make the same mistakes again.

I have also discovered that sometimes the consequences of our past sins will come back later on in life and we will have to deal with them. However, if we trust in God and His love, He will always direct our paths and help us deal with whatever comes our way. The Bible is true when it says that if we trust in God, He will work all things together for our good.

Living with the Consequences of Our Sin

Without a doubt, the hardest thing that I had to deal with at that time in my life was my wife's decision to end our marriage and not to reconcile. As much as I did not want it to happen, my wife soon moved with our children to another part of Canada and eventually married someone else.

I cannot blame my wife or think badly of her for doing this. It was not her evil behavior that had caused our marriage to fail. It was mine. I know that I had hurt her too deeply, and she was unable to cope with having me back into her life or in the lives of our children. I also knew that I had no right to judge my wife for leaving me to be with another man. We had done almost exactly the same thing to her first husband when I had moved in with her in the beginning of our relationship, while she was still married.

Do you remember what I said about having to deal with the consequences of our past sins? I understood that as a result of my previous sin, God was now causing me to experience the heartache and sorrow that my wife's first husband had suffered when another man (me) came in and took away his wife and children from him. The Word of God says that we reap what we sow, and this was the most painful lesson of all for me to learn. I did not want to ever make the same mistake again. Consequently, it would take thirteen years and a whole lot of spiritual growth before God would open the door for me to marry again, but this time it was with Jesus and the Holy Spirit at the helm of my life.

13

Are God's Ways Unjust?

What Kind of God Would Allow Murderers, Rapists, and Child Molesters into Heaven?

The truth is that God does not allow such people into heaven. God will not allow anyone into heaven who is still walking an evil path when they die. Who deserves to go to heaven, and who does not? The real question in many people's minds is, "What right does God have to love and bless people who have such an evil past, just because they repent, and yet He will reject me when I have been a decent, hardworking person all of my life? It's just not fair!"

People sometimes express offense and indignation at the idea that God could ever love and forgive people who were once such great sinners and have later repented. In their minds, such people deserve to be punished, and punished greatly, for their sins. However, they think that they deserve to be forgiven for their own sins, because their sins have not been so "bad." As a matter of fact, the sin of pride is at the forefront in the hearts of those who reject God because they refuse to admit that they are sinners and in need of salvation when the Word of God clearly states that all have sinned and fallen short of God's goodness. How ready we are to judge and condemn others for their sins, while we so easily excuse our own wickedness.

Evil Is a Deadly, Blinding Poison

Jesus and the apostles ran into this kind of reasoning in their day, and obviously the same vain concept of entitlement still exists in our day. People are still denying God's Word. They are still rejecting God and believing the lie that continuing to embrace the knowledge of good and evil will "earn" us the future of becoming like "gods."

God's Word explains to us that this was the kind of thinking that once led to such corruption of human society that mankind's every thought eventually became wicked and the whole world had to be destroyed with the Flood. The aftermath gave future generations of mankind another opportunity to follow the truth.

None of us wants to believe that it is possible for mankind to eventually become so embedded with evil that there is no good at all left in us. We don't want to believe that we could ever become murderers, yet our generation is already killing unborn babies by the millions, and every day millions more people around the world are dying through violence and neglect.

The crazy thing is that this "end times" generation is once again quickly headed toward the same levels of violence and immorality that existed in Noah's day—but we don't see it! The world still refuses to believe God, nor do they choose to turn back to Him.

Jesus Died for All

Either Jesus Christ has the desire and the power to forgive us and cleanse us of every sin, or He does not have the ability to forgive any sin at all. God did not offer up His beloved Son to die on the cross only for your sin or my sin. Jesus Christ suffered and died so that every single sinner who repents and believes in Jesus Christ could be forgiven and come back to their Father God.

> *For the message of the cross is foolishness to those who are perishing, but to us who are being saved it is the power of God. For it is written: "I will destroy the wisdom of the wise; the intelligence of the intelligent I will frustrate." Where is the wise person? Where is the teacher of the law? Where is the philosopher of this age?*
>
> *Has not God made foolish the wisdom of the world? For since in the wisdom of God the world through its wisdom did not know him, God was pleased through the foolishness of what was preached to save those who believe. Jews demand signs and Greeks look for wisdom, but we preach Christ crucified: a stumbling block to Jews and foolishness to Gentiles, but to those whom God has called, both Jews and Greeks, Christ the power of God and the wisdom of God* (1 Corinthians 1:18–24 NIV).

Don't let this wonderful example of undeserved love become a stumbling block to you. The apostle Paul explains to us that the religious crowds become offended and that the unbelievers think it is all nonsense when we preach that the death of Jesus Christ paid the price for the redemption of all who repent and believe on Him for salvation—but it is true nonetheless.

Have you done your best to serve God all your life? Good for you! God loves you, and everything He has is yours to share. But you also have to realize that God loves all of His children. He loves the ones who have gone down to terrible depths of depravity just as much as He loves you. That is why, when they repent, God embraces them and receives them back with forgiveness, mercy, and great joy.

That is why I know that God has forgiven me, now that I have come back to Him. Like the prodigal son in the Bible, I know that I once squandered my life away, but God never stopped loving me and waiting for me to come back to Him. Now that I am back, I don't ever want to leave again. Why would I ever go back to the devil, the cruel stepfather who nearly destroyed my life?

Confession and Forgiveness

True Christianity teaches that we must repent of our sins, and this sometimes involves confessing our guilt to the ones we have sinned against and doing our best to make reparations to our victims.

Under certain circumstances, we may also be required to confess our sin to the Church, as well. For example, a person in leadership who has been involved in illegal or immoral activities may be required to confess and repent of their sin before the Body of Christ in order to emphasize that such behavior is evil and unacceptable conduct for Christians.

In addition to this, the Word of God instructs that all professing Christians—including leaders—who refuse to repent of following after evil must be confronted by the Church. If they still refuse to repent, they must be rejected from the fellowship until they change their ways. Sinners may view this as harsh and unloving, but that is because they love their sin more than they love God.

Should the Church Protect Those Who Continue to Practice Evil?

Such a vile concept should never exist in the Church, and yet it does exist in many churches throughout the world today. The idea that an unrepentant person can go into a church and confess their sin to a priest or pastor and then be absolved of their guilt, without ever truly repenting of their sin, is an abomination to the Lord.

Christian ministers who become aware of things like theft and adultery and rape and child abuse and violence and murder—and then proceed to cover it up and allow it to continue under the unbiblical philosophy of confidentiality—are sinners. They will one day be judged by God for their evil, and they will be considered just as guilty as if they had committed the crime themselves.

The proper conduct for ministers in these situations is to do their best to convince the offender to repent and face the consequences for the evil that they have done. If they refuse to voluntarily repent, they must be turned over to the authorities to be judged, just as you would with any other criminal. Only a fool would think that God will not judge the evil behavior that goes on within some church circles, hiding behind perversions of the concepts of confidentiality and sanctuary.

Are Christians Above the Law?

Of course not! The law exists to be a terror to all evildoers, including professing Christians. If you think that you can profess Christianity in order to keep yourself out of jail, or use it as a "get out of jail free" card when you should rightfully be incarcerated, you are deceiving yourself.

God brought the law into existence because of unrighteousness, and the professing Christian who is involved in criminal activities is just as deserving of criminal prosecution as the avowed unbeliever. Don't be confused about the difference between forgiveness and justice. God forgives the repentant sinner, but that does not mean that we will necessarily be spared from the legal consequences for the sins that we have committed. Jesus forgave the repentant thief on the cross for his life of sin, but the man did not escape the suffering and death that was the legal consequence for his transgressions.

Why is it that so many professing Christians are able to fantasize about going to jail or suffering for their faith—and yet they are abhorred at the idea that they might deserve to be in jail for their evil behavior? The Word of God tells us that if we suffer for righteousness' sake there is a reward, but if we suffer for our own faults and sins, we should realize that if we have done the crime, we deserve to serve the time and we should do so without complaining.

Where Is the Justice for the Victims?

Why should those who are guilty of horrendous sins in their past be allowed into heaven? The Word of God does have an answer to this question, but whether or not it makes sense to you will depend on what you choose to believe regarding the history and future of the human race.

Are you are a person who believes that mankind is nothing more than randomly evolved creatures who originated from pond slime and apes? Are we beings without design or purpose? Do you believe that human beings will all one day die and simply cease to exist, as the evolutionists teach? If you embrace these false beliefs, they will cloud your understanding of how

God is able to recompense the innocent who suffer during this lifetime.

The apostle Paul once said that if our fragile, natural lifespan is the only thing that mankind has to look forward to, for many people life would be little more than a hopeless and miserable existence. Undeserved suffering covers the entire planet, and if this life is all there is, many people would be better off if they had never even been born.

On the other hand, if we choose to believe God's promise that we are all spiritual beings who will only live out the first tiny fraction of our eternal lives in these mortal bodies, our perspective on life and the things that we suffer in this life will change immensely.

Life on earth can be cruel at times, but God promises that He has all eternity to make up for any and all unjust suffering that every human being on earth endures during their natural lifespan on this planet. God even promises that one day He will erase all pain and sorrow from the hearts of those who love Him. Even the memory of former evils will be forgotten.

When God's love is so unfathomable that He is willing to forgive and pardon the greatest of sinners when they repent, do you not realize that God will be even more motivated to provide love, healing, comfort, and eternal compensation to those who have innocently suffered evil during their lives here on earth? God is extremely good, and His mercy endures forever. He will not fail to heal the suffering of the innocent victims.

14

Traveling a New Path

God Heals Old Family Wounds

Some sins cannot be undone. As much as I wanted to be reconciled to my wife and children, my marriage was unrecoverable—but God did help me in many other ways. My mother and I had not been close for years. Until that point in my life, I had not treated my mother very well, due to deep-seated resentments regarding her alcoholism that went far back into my childhood. In fact, the last memory that I have of my mother before my own life fell apart was the previous March, when Mom had phoned to invite us all to Easter dinner. I had agreed to attend, but I warned Mom that we would not stay if she was drunk when we arrived.

The moment that we pulled into the driveway and she came out to greet us, there was no mistaking the slurred speech and the wobbly stance. Mom was bombed again. I told her that we were leaving and we never even got out of the car. She grabbed on to the door handle, begging me to stay, but I was so angry and my heart was so hardened that I continued to back out of the driveway with her holding on to the door handle, dragging her along as I went until she couldn't hold on any longer and she fell into the dirt.

That event took place thirty-five years ago, and I can still see that picture in my mind. When I reflect on the fact that I had considered myself a Christian at the time, it is evidence of just how deluded I was during that point in my life. On top of all these things, while God was dealing with me in Williams Lake, I had missed my own stepfather's funeral, leaving Mom to deal with everything all by herself when she needed me the most—yet God had a plan in place to allow me to make up for my past shortcomings.

A New Creature in Christ Jesus

I was a different person when I came back from Williams Lake. God had opened my eyes to see that my mom's sins were no worse than my own. I understood now that they were only different from mine, and it gave me a love and a compassion for her that I had never had before. I told Mom everything that had happened to cause the breakup of my marriage, and how sorry I was for the way I had been treating her and for not being there to support her at Dad's funeral. I told her all about my encounter with God in Williams Lake, and that I was now determined to truly live for God for the rest of my life.

The end result was that, although Mom was somewhat shocked by everything that I said to her, she told me that she had been struggling with depression and loneliness now that Dad was gone, and she offered to let me stay with her until I could find a place of my own, as long as I didn't start preaching to her.

I laughed about that and agreed to her terms. I didn't have to preach to her. This was the start of a reconciliation between myself and my mother that would culminate with her badly wanting what I now had. In her own time, Mom too accepted Jesus as her Savior and was delivered from her own addictions. Our last dozen years together would finally bring about the loving family relationship that had long been missing from both of our lives.

Years afterward, when we talked about that first day, Mom said that she wasn't sure at first whether or not I had gone over the deep end, but she knew something was definitely different about me when I came back. I knew that too. Finally, I knew what it was to be born again and to have God as my Father.

The Many Faces of Christian Charity

One thing that I learned during that period of my life is that true Christian charity has nothing to do with what group or denomination to which you belong. Whereas years ago, Mom had encountered professing Christians who were unwilling even to bury her dead, this time around both church and community stepped up to help a grieving low-income pensioner in need.

Some people are fortunate enough to have a financial nest egg when someone dies, but Dad's insurance company had gone bankrupt a year before he died. Instead of an inheritance of any kind, Dad's sinful lifestyle had left Mom with six months' back rent that had accumulated against their rental home while Dad was in the hospital. Things were not good financially, but God saw her need.

I found out after my return to our hometown that, since my stepfather was an ex-serviceman, the local Legion had graciously covered Dad's funeral costs. Also, the United Church minister had volunteered to perform the funeral service for Mom. In addition, the rental home in which Mom and Dad had been living was owned by the company that Dad had been working for when he became ill. It was a relief that they were compassionate enough to cancel the owed back rent when he passed away.

As for me, upon returning home I was not comfortable going to my former minister for counsel, since his wife had gained a reputation for sharing intimate details of people's lives with others through gossip. Therefore, I approached the pastor of a local Baptist church and found him to be a kind and devout man who was a great help to me. He agreed to counsel me whenever I felt I needed someone to talk to, even though I was attending another church of a different denomination at the time.

At the time of the breakup of my marriage, my lawyer had urged me to fight for half of everything, but I now believed that the right thing for me to do was to care for my wife and children, whether she wanted to stay with me or not. Therefore, I gave all of our assets and the family car to my wife for the present and future needs of her and the children.

My lawyer thought that I was doing this because of lingering feelings of guilt, but I actually was not. I knew that if I did the right thing, God would take care of my own needs. He did, but that didn't happen overnight. Upon my return to my hometown, I was completely broke—worse than broke. I was deeply in debt, with no money, no assets, no job, and no transportation.

God Begins to Open Doors for Me

The local lumber economy was still in a nosedive, and I was not expecting much success at job hunting, but when I went to apply at the local sawmill where I had worked years before, the hiring person recognized me, and he turned out to be someone who had been a good friend of my stepdad's. In spite of the economic slump in our town, I was hired immediately to go back to the well-paying lumber-grading job that I had left years before.

I had to hitchhike to work for the first couple of paychecks, but soon I had saved up six hundred dollars to purchase a decent used car.

Then the pastor of the local Pentecostal church offered to lease to me a one-bedroom cabin, which had been the former pastorate, charging me only a very nominal amount of rent. After talking things over with Mom and determining that she would be okay with living on her own, I moved into my own place. I was overjoyed when a friend gave me a little gray kitten as a housewarming gift. At least I would have a pet to keep me company as I continued to mourn the loss of my wife and children from my life. Things were starting to get a little better, but you never know when there might be more heartache coming in your life—just around the corner.

God's Mercy in the Form of a Tortoiseshell Cat

If anyone ever tries to tell you that becoming a Christian is all good times, lollipops, and rainbows, they are mistaken. God does some wonderful things in the lives of believers, but that does not mean that there will be no more trials and tribulations in our lives. God never promised that this life would always be fair or pleasant. What He has promised is that if we trust in Him, He will help us get through whatever adversities come our way.

God also tells us that if we have sinned and then suffer for it, we should do so without complaining, but if we innocently suffer for things that are not our own fault, in time the suffering will pass and God has all eternity to recompense us for any suffering that we have endured that was not of our own causing.

My first setback occurred only a few days after I moved into the cabin. I woke up in the morning to find that the beautiful little kitten that I had been given was dead in its bed. This crushed me. It tore my heart out. I wailed and suffered over the death of that little creature, just as much as I had over my own family leaving me. As I went through this grief, Satan, the accuser, was telling me how worthless and terrible I was. I could not keep a wife. I could not take care of my children. What kind of person or even what type of Christian was I that I couldn't even successfully care for a kitten?

The whole incident was devastating to me, but after a long, hard cry I calmed down enough to return to my trust in God and begin to reject Satan's attacks. The truth was that this was just one of those things that happen in life and we have no explanations for it. If anyone had killed the kitten, it was Satan, not me and certainly not God. God reminded me that it was okay to mourn for the kitten, but that I was not responsible for its death. Satan is, after all, the angel who holds the power of death.

Eventually I regained my composure enough that I decided to go and sit in the sun on the front steps. It was a beautiful, warm day, and as I was sitting there, a fully grown tortoiseshell cat came up and started rubbing against me and purring. This comforted me quite a bit. It was like God was saying to me that everything was going to be okay, and we just sat there enjoying each other's company for quite a while.

Then, when I got up to go back into the cabin, the cat waltzed right in and made herself at home. For the next four years, this cat would be my constant companion and comforter. She followed me everywhere, even when I went on hikes through the fields. She remained with me until I was well into my second year at Bible college and strong enough to make it on my own. Thank You, Jesus, for the gift of the tortoiseshell cat.

Learning to Trust God

In the beginning of my new life, I had no vehicle, so I had to hitchhike to work, but after a few months I managed to scrape together six hundred dollars to buy a decent used car. I really appreciated that car, and it was important to me. There was no bus service in our town, and my work was about five miles from where I lived. If I could not carpool with someone, my only other viable alternative was hitchhiking or walking the entire five miles.

When I arrived at church one Sunday afternoon, there was a widow in the congregation whose car had broken down and was not repairable. Because she lived out of town and had small children, an appeal was made to the congregation for anyone who had an extra car that she would be able to borrow until her family could afford to purchase another vehicle. Right away, I heard God say, "Give her your car!"

In a fine example of my spiritual generosity and maturity, my first response was, "God, I don't want to have to hitchhike again!" So I waited for someone else to step up and volunteer their vehicle, but no one else did, and the Lord repeated Himself, adding, "Who do you love more, Me or your car? Do you love this woman, or your car? Give her the car!" That was enough for me. I handed the keys to her, explaining that God had told me to give the car to her—and she was very grateful. It felt good, regardless of the inconvenience that it was going to be for me to have to hitchhike again until I could afford another car. A short time later, we signed the papers and the car became hers.

I was fully prepared to have to go back to hitchhiking to work for quite a while until I could afford another car, but later that week I happened to be walking past the GM dealership and I noticed that they were loading vehicles onto a car-hauling trailer. I spotted a nearly new Datsun pickup in the line waiting to be loaded, and I felt led by the Lord to stop and ask them about the truck. The owner of the dealership told me that they had not been able to sell the vehicle, so it was on its way to another location.

Then the man asked me if I was interested, and he offered me a very good below-market price on the truck. When I explained to him that I really liked the truck but that I had just gotten back to work so I did not have the cash and was pretty sure that I would be unable to get any financing for it, the owner took me back into his office, sold me the truck on the spot, and took care of the financing himself at a very reasonable rate. So the end result of it all was that I had given my twenty-year-old, six-hundred-dollar car to God, and He had replaced it with a very nice pickup less than two years old at a very reasonable price and with low payments. Listening to God had turned out to be not so bad of a decision after all!

God Provides Wood

I have experienced many examples of God's provision over the years since those days, but another that stands out during those early days of serving God involves a middle-aged, godly Christian woman whose husband had abandoned her. She was unable to work because of her poor health and she was living in a terrible little shack in the middle of town. Her only source of heat or means to cook were two woodstoves in a climate that could reach forty degrees below zero in the wintertime.

To make matters worse, her roof leaked like a sieve when it rained, and her landlord refused to do anything about fixing the old tar-paper roofing over her house. After visiting her one rainy day and seeing the pots scattered around the kitchen to catch the water as it was coming through the holes in the roof, God impressed me to help the woman.

Winter was coming on, so firewood was the first priority. All of my extra money was going to pay down my debt load, so I didn't have the money to buy any firewood for her, but I had a chainsaw and a splitting ax, so I prayed to God that if He would help me find the wood, I would split it and stack enough of it to get her through the winter. After all, I now had a nice pickup to haul it in.

Sometimes I would have to find a fallen tree in the bush and cut it up when her supply was getting low, but God certainly came through on His end. More often than not that winter, I was simply able to find wood in the form of fenceposts or precut firewood that people left at the dump. There were other times when people who had heard about her need would give wood to me, and all I would have to do was simply haul it over to her house.

Before the winter was over, the Lord had helped me provide over twenty cords of wood for her, enough for the coming winter and the next one. (For those of you who don't know what a "cord" of wood is, it's a stack of wood four feet high by four feet wide by eight feet long.) God came through big-time.

God Provides a Roof

Although I felt good about being able to provide wood for this woman, a new roof was a whole other matter. One of the local churches had offered to donate some extra tar and roofing nails to the cause if they were needed, but all of the other roofing materials and labor are expensive, and extra money was the one thing that I did not have. I had made a commitment to the Lord to pay off the thirty-thousand-dollar debt from my business collapse that I still owed to creditors. All of my spare money was being put toward paying down that debt, but God had another way to solve the problem.

One day, as I was up at the dump looking for firewood, something unusual caught my eye. It was four large rolls about four feet wide and three feet around. When I got closer, I could see that these were rolls of used rubber conveyor belting that someone had discarded—waterproof rolls. Right away I knew that I had found the roofing material for the woman's old shack. The next problem was to figure out how to get them into the truck by myself because each roll was perhaps thirty feet long and weighed hundreds of pounds. After a lot of prayer, muscle, and improvised levers, I finally got them into the truck and contacted some men from our church to help put the roofing up for her.

The guys were astounded that I had managed to get the conveyor belting into the truck by myself. It had to have been with God's help because afterward it took three of us to get each roll down and out of the truck. Fortunately, the shack was quite small and the conveyor belting was long enough to go over the peak of the roof and down to the eaves on both sides of the house. All we had to do was seal the seams between the belts with the tar and roofing nails.

Then, when we got down to our last piece, we ran out of nails, and not one of us had enough money to buy any more, but God knew how to take care of that problem, too. While we were trying to figure out what to do next, one of the non-Christians whom I knew from work recognized me as he was walking by and asked what we were up to. I explained to him what we were doing and our dilemma of now being out of roofing nails and not having any money to buy any more.

"I can take care of that," he said, and about ten minutes later he came back with enough nails from the hardware store to finish the job. Thank You, Jesus! In the next rainstorm, the lady was elated to say that there were no more leaks, and I would venture to say that in the end, the roof covering that we installed probably outlasted the rest of that dilapidated old shack.

15

Assembling Together

Small Church, Big Vision

God's Word says that Christians should not forsake the regular gathering together for fellowship, worship, teaching, and prayer, so another thing that I did after returning to my hometown was to commit to regular church attendance, Bible reading, and prayer, and I do mean commit. On Wednesday nights, Sunday mornings, and Sunday evenings, I returned to attending my former church.

In addition to that, during the years before my own crisis, I had crossed paths a few times with members of another small church. They had struck me as a little fanatical at the time because of their exuberance and boldness about sharing Jesus with others. But now I was interested in what they had to say, so I started attending their church, as well, which worked out perfectly because they met on Sunday afternoons, Tuesday evenings, and Saturday nights.

If you think that six church services a week could be way too excessive, try to understand that until that period in my life, my time had been filled with family, pornography, drugs, booze, and other assorted sinful behaviors of numerous kinds—and now that was all gone. There was a huge hole in my life, and God wanted to keep me in constant contact and fellowship with His people and His presence until I was strong enough to stand on my own. I never found these church services to be a burden. I was thirsty for God. I needed the teaching and the fellowship at the time, and I thrived on it for the first two years back at home. It was certainly much better than sitting in my cabin alone or getting caught up again in all of the things that had gotten me into trouble in the first place.

Let me tell you a little about the two churches that I was attending at that time. The first had started out in a tiny building with a pastor who had a vision of ministering to the city by contacting everyone in town and offering to send a bus around to pick up their children. Every Sunday morning, the bus would be sent out to take kids to Sunday school and then back home again afterward. God was behind the idea. Before long, they had to build a bigger church—a much bigger church—because many of the parents of the children had begun attending, as well.

Then something happened that happens in many denominational churches. Someone "up the ladder" decided to send this successful pastor and his wife off to try to resurrect another struggling church in a different city. They were replaced by a pastor who did not know the people and who had little idea of the vision upon which the local assembly had been founded. This new older pastor had education and experience, but he did not have the anointing. People began to lose interest, and attendance was waning by the time I started to attend regularly again. Even though it was theoretically a charismatic church, the services were often lacking in spirit. They were dry and lifeless. I continued to attend there more out of loyalty to the denomination and loyalty to God than out of actually enjoying and growing from the teaching I was receiving there. I was looking for something more out of my Christianity.

Then there was the other church. They were seen as real radicals because they would go around town handing out tracts and talking to people about repentance and Jesus. The senior pastor was also a woman, and that was frowned upon by some. Others even referred to these believers as a cult, although that was not the impression that I had gotten from previous encounters with them. To me, they had seemed like genuine Christians, so I decided to check them out.

Small Church, Big Anointing

Ironically, this was the group who had moved into the small building that the first church had abandoned when they moved into their larger facilities, and the meetings of this group were a whole different brand of Christianity. These people were on fire for God!

I doubt whether the place could have seated more than fifty people. I remember that the average service had about thirty people or less in attendance, and when the praise and worship team was called up, sometimes a third of the congregation were up at the front ministering in music and song to God and to the rest of the people. The congregation wasn't shy about joining in when it was time to worship, either. It was definitely a lively, joyful, and prayerful place of worship.

The services were planned and orderly, but they were not so rigid that there was no allowance for God to guide the direction and spirit of the meetings. The congregation was encouraged to participate and contribute any input as they felt God leading them, all under the guidance, leadership, and authority of the pastor and the elders.

Usually, but not always, the meetings would follow a planned schedule and there would be a snack and beverages afterward. Sometimes, however, there would be such a presence of God in the service that the praise and worship of God would continue for most of the meeting and would include spontaneous, unrehearsed praise and prayer from some of those in attendance.

I soon found out that these people knew how to pray. They didn't pray prayers from a book. They prayed to God, not to anybody else listening. They prayed with purpose and abandonment and faith that their prayers would be answered, and let me tell you, some pretty miraculous things happened while I was attending that little church.

Furthermore, their preaching and teaching was solid, biblical, and supported by the Word of God. It was like water for my thirst and bread for my hunger. This little church put meat on my dry bones and helped me grow quickly in the Word of God. They were also my first real exposure to what the Bible refers to as the baptism of the Holy Spirit and speaking in tongues. They provided good, balanced teaching from the Word of God to help me understand that the gifts and ministry of the Holy Spirit are still available and valuable to Christians today.

I was actually content to continue to attend and learn from both of these churches. I saw no harm in doing this. As far as I was concerned, we were all Christians, but about two years after accepting Christ, the pastor of the larger church suggested that I shouldn't be dividing my loyalties between two different churches. So I took his advice and stopped going to his church—much to his surprise, I am sure.

16

Modern Miracles?

God Is a God of the Impossible

There are many people in the world and in the Church today who have trouble believing that God still performs healings and miracles in our day and age, but He certainly does. I definitely know what the Bible has to say about the subject:

> *Later Jesus appeared to the Eleven as they were eating; he rebuked them for their lack of faith and their stubborn refusal to believe those who had seen him after he had risen. He said to them, "Go into all the world and preach the gospel to all creation. Whoever believes and is baptized will be saved, but whoever does not believe will be condemned. And these signs will accompany those who believe: In my name they will drive out demons; they will speak in new tongues; they will pick up snakes with their hands; and when they drink deadly poison, it will not hurt them at all; they will place their hands on sick people, and they will get well." After the Lord Jesus had spoken to them, he was taken up into heaven and he sat at the right hand of God. Then the disciples went out and preached everywhere, and the Lord worked with them and confirmed his word by the signs that accompanied it* (Mark 16:14–20 NIV).

> *Once when he was eating with them, he commanded them, "Do not leave Jerusalem until the Father sends you the gift he promised, as I told you before. John baptized with water, but in just a few days you will be baptized with the Holy Spirit." So when the apostles were with Jesus, they kept asking him, "Lord, has the time come for you to free Israel and restore our kingdom?" He replied, "The Father alone has the authority to set those dates and times, and they are not for you to know. But you will receive power when the Holy Spirit comes upon you. And you will be my witnesses, telling people about me everywhere—in Jerusalem, throughout Judea, in Samaria, and to the ends of the earth." After saying this, he was taken up into a cloud while they were watching, and they could no longer see him* (Acts 1:4–9 NLT).

This is a great passage describing God's promise to move through Christians in miraculous ways. As I continued studying the New Testament about the accounts of Peter and Stephen and Philip and Paul and John, all moving in the realm of the gifts and power of the Holy Spirit, I began to question the arguments of those who claimed that God no longer wants to move in this way through Christians.

I began to wonder whether maybe God does continue to move in these ways in the lives of those who choose to believe that God will do this. I began to believe that God wanted to move this way in my own life. As I began to ask God to do such things and believed that He would do what He said He would do, I also began to experience the truth that the gifts of the Holy Spirit are still available to us after all.

God Still Responds to Faith

Jesus made several remarkable statements to His disciples during His time on earth:

> *"I tell you the truth, anyone who believes in me will do the same works I have done, and even greater works, because I am going to be with the Father. You can ask for anything in my name, and I will do it, so that the Son can bring glory to the Father. Yes, ask me for anything in my name, and I will do it! "If you love me, obey my commandments. And I will ask the Father, and he will give you another Advocate, who will never leave you. He is the Holy Spirit, who leads into all truth. The world cannot receive him, because it isn't looking for him and doesn't recognize him. But you know him, because he lives with you now and later will be in you"* (John 14:12–17 NLT).

> *Jesus replied, "Truly I tell you, if you have faith and do not doubt, not only can you do what was done to the fig tree, but also you can say to this mountain, 'Go, throw yourself into the sea,' and it will be done. If you believe, you will receive whatever you ask for in prayer"* (Matthew 21:21–22 NIV).

All of these biblical passages in the Gospels and Acts bring us to the following questions. Can the Word of God be trusted? Is the Word of God true or not true? Is there any evidence to suggest that God still moves in these ways today? Well, yes, there is!

In addition to studying the Bible itself, during this period of my life I also spent a considerable amount of time reading books about some of the pioneers of the Christian faith in North

America and elsewhere. I learned about people like the Wesley brothers, Jonathan Edwards, Charles Finney, Smith Wigglesworth, A.A. Alan, Aimee Semple McPherson, Katherine Kuhlman, and numerous others who all told of wonderful examples of God moving in miraculous power in response to prayer.

Then, among my generation, there were those who were on TV at the time who were also proclaiming that God still moves in the miraculous in our generation—ministers like Oral Roberts, Joel Osteen, Jimmy Swaggart, Jim and Tammy Faye Bakker, John Hagee, Benny Hinn, Peter Popoff, Rex Humbard, Ernest Angley, Marilyn Hickey, Joyce Meyer, Paula White, and the list goes on and on.

Before you object to some of the people whom I have included in the above list and complain about some of those whom I have left out, listen to what the Word of God has to say about God's gifts and calling:

> *God's gifts and God's call are under full warranty—never canceled, never rescinded. There was a time not so long ago when you were on the outs with God. But then the Jews slammed the door on him and things opened up for you. Now they are on the outs. But with the door held wide open for you, they have a way back in. In one way or another, God makes sure that we all experience what it means to be outside so that he can personally open the door and welcome us back in* (Romans 11:29–32 MSG).

I'm sorry if I might have left out some of your favorites, and yes, some of these men and women of God whom I did mention have had ethical and moral failures in some areas of their lives and have had to face serious repercussions for their sins, but that does not repudiate the promises of God about what He is willing to do if people have faith to believe. God responds to His people stepping out in faith, regardless of the fact that we as human beings are not perfect and that we are prone to stumbling.

All throughout the Bible, we can see examples of God greatly using people who were flawed and imperfect, yet God still used them in proportion to the faith that they had to believe the particular promises of God. Samson was a perfect example of someone whom God used for a time to perform mighty deeds, even though his personal life was a mess. Samson paid with his life for his sins in the end, but he was still used mightily by God in the areas where he had faith to believe in God's promises.

Held Back by Vanity

The greatest stumbling blocks to believing that God still moves in signs and wonders today are vanity and self-righteousness. I hear people point to the imperfections and failures in the lives of some of these ministers and declare, "See, I told you that it was all of the devil." This kind of attitude is not of God. If we allow ourselves to be led astray by our own vanities and perceptions of being better than others, we will become distracted and offended when God uses other people whom we perceive to be flawed and imperfect.

I have news for you: We are all flawed and imperfect! If our faith is in a man or a woman and we focus on human performance, we will always end up disappointed and doubting God. When some of the greatest televangelists were discovered to have human flaws just like the rest of us, there were some who suddenly rejected everything about their teachings and turned away from God because all their faith was tied up in these human beings. They had elevated the ministers and ministries into God's place. Then they were devastated when they discovered that these people were only human, subject to the same temptations and failures as the rest of us.

The truth is that God does not use people because they are flawless but because they have faith to believe the Lord. When we are willing to step out in faith, God promises to honor that faith. When some of the greatest and most famous televangelists were knocked from their pedestals, it did not destroy my faith in God's Word. It instead confirmed to me that what God had told me was true.

When the hidden sins of some of the televangelists exploded onto the TV and the pages of the tabloid newspapers, it did not destroy my faith because my faith was not in the televangelists. It instead inspired me to write a Christian tract, warning myself and all others to make sure that we do not retain areas of unrepentance in our lives after we come to Jesus. We cannot have one foot in Christianity and one foot in unrepentance and not have our worlds collapse around us.

I presented the tract to one of the largest tract publishers in Canada, and they saw the merit in the message. They published it for free, and since that day tens of thousands of those tracts have been distributed throughout the world. I have no way of knowing how many people were influenced by that little tract, but I know it was the truth and that God was in it.

Before we start throwing stones at other people, we need to look at our own lives. When Christian ministers and ministries fail, we shouldn't be throwing rocks at them. We should be praying that God will bring them to repentance. Neither should it destroy our faith in God's Word. It should instead serve as a warning to us to take a good look at our own lives and heed the apostle Paul's message to himself and every other professing Christian:

> *So I run with purpose in every step. I am not just shadow-boxing. I discipline my body like an athlete, training it to do what it should. Otherwise, I fear that after preaching to others I myself might be disqualified* (1 Corinthians 9:26–27 NLT).

Paul's message is clear: Don't get so caught up in preaching to others that you forget that you must keep your own thoughts, words, and actions disciplined in order to serve Jesus. It is not enough to proclaim that Jesus is Lord. None of us wants to be in the position where we are one day crying out to Jesus to open the door and let us in, only to hear Jesus say, "Sorry, you are disqualified, you cheater. Depart from Me, you evildoer and worker of iniquity."

17

God Is Still Alive

Signs and Wonders

I wanted to know. Does God still move in this way today? My first exposure to such things actually happened during the early seventies, before I ever truly repented. One of the things that motivated me to learn more about God's healing power was that my first wife's father had been a professing Christian who loved to watch a certain famous healing televangelist on TV.

After watching the program at his house, I soon become a regular viewer of the services at home. I was fascinated and sometimes brought to tears by the programs that showed adults and children being healed. I used to wonder and hope that this could possibly be genuine and not just more of the charlatanism that was being exposed as occurring in some Christian ministries at the time.

Then my father-in-law became the victim of a rapidly advancing stomach cancer. He was dying, he was in constant agony, and the doctors could do little to help him. At the time, I was still walking in disobedience to God. I was not ready to completely repent and obey God in my own life, but I was stirred with compassion for this man whom I cared for deeply. When I heard on the TV program that it was possible to go to the man of God and be prayed for "in proxy" for someone else's needs, I felt that if there was any chance that this would help my father-in-law, I needed to try this for him.

If you are unfamiliar with the term "in proxy," it means that you can go to another believer for prayer, not for yourself, but for someone else's needs. The man or woman of God then prays for that person's need, laying their hands on you to transfer the power of God to you. Then you return to lay hands on the ailing person and pray for their need, trusting in God to answer the prayer.

Hoping for the Power of God

I was honestly desiring to help my father-in-law, yet I was also seriously searching for something to convince me that the power of God was still present in the world today. This was not a small venture for me. Even though I was not a true believer yet, I was a sincere seeker of God. My quest would require a four-thousand-kilometer flight to the eastern United States to visit the home church of a minister whom I had only ever seen on television before this time.

As far as the preacher goes, his name is unimportant, and there was nothing about the man's appearance that would draw a person to him. He did not have the classic he-man physique or good looks that many TV ministers have. He was short, a little overweight, and had a rather comical, squeaky voice, but something about the book that he had written and his TV program suggested to me that this was a man who did his best to walk with God.

I showed up an hour early to make sure that I would get a good seat for the service, and I was quite surprised to find that this only put me fairly close to the front of what would turn out to be a very long lineup—just to get into the church. It was a huge building compared to what I was used to seeing, and the seating consisted of long, wooden pews capable of seating twenty or more people per row with perhaps four or five aisles between the rows. I settled myself into a center pew a few rows from the front and waited for the service to start.

Right from the time that the service began, the air was charged with spiritual energy and an air of expectation from many of those who were in attendance. The praise and worship flowed like water rising and falling in a wonderful way for quite a while, until it was time for the announcements, the offering, and the message of the day. The sermon was centered on repentance, faith in Jesus Christ, and the scriptural promise that God is the same yesterday, today, and forever. Soon the main message was over, and then the invitation was given for prayer. The minister encouraged everyone to remain respectful, reverent, and prayerful for the needs of those to whom he was ministering. A few people left after the sermon, but most stayed and I could see that many were praying.

The front rows had been reserved for those with crutches, wheelchairs, and other special needs, so these were the first to be prayed for, but they were soon joined by other people streaming to the front from every aisle. Sometimes the minister would stop what he was doing and go out into the middle of the congregation to pray for a particular person. For the first few minutes, nothing at all unusual happened—but then it all started.

Experiencing the Power of God

The man of God continued to be faithful to pray for people without any apparent results. Some of them fell to the floor and lay there for a while, and others simply returned to their seats after being prayed for and that was all that happened.

But then one young couple brought their preschool daughter forward, explaining that she was deaf and dumb and had not spoken since her birth. The minister put his fingers in the child's ears and commanded the deaf and dumb spirit to come out of the girl and never bother her again, and then he leaned over and spoke into the girl's ear the word "baby" and the child repeated the word. Then he spoke into the other ear, and the child said it again. Then he stood behind the girl where she could not see him and said the word again.

The child immediately jumped and clapped her hands as she said the word "baby" one more time, and the child's parents were immediately overcome with years of pent-up emotion as they realized what had just happened. I could tell by the reaction of the child and the parents that this was genuine. This was real, and the whole congregation began to shout and praise God as the minister continued to pray for other people—and that was only the beginning.

Soon others began to be healed. Blind people were seeing. Others who were deaf and dumb were praising God. Crutches were being thrown down, and people who obviously had not even had the power to stand for years were getting up out of their wheelchairs and walking and then running around the place.

God Touches Me

There was one thing that bothered me about all of this. Sometimes during the prayer time, the minister would warn someone to repent of ongoing sin in their life, and that frightened me, because I knew that my life was not right before God. I wanted to go forward for prayer for my father-in-law, but I was too afraid of being exposed in front of everyone there as a sinner to go forward to the altar. Yet I also desperately wanted to believe in God.

I was praying with all my might that God would speak to me and help me believe in Him. I also prayed that God would have mercy on my father-in-law and use me to pray for him. I had my eyes closed as tightly as I could, and I was praying with such intensity that I was literally shaking.

Gradually, I began to realize that it was not just me who was shaking. I could hear a loud and powerful rattling noise. Virtually the whole congregation had been standing during the prayer time. I was also standing at the end seat of my row, and I had been holding on to the pew in front of me all the time I was praying. When I opened my eyes, I could see the people around me looking at me and the pew that I was holding on to. No one else was touching the pew, and yet the entire pew was vibrating and rattling up and down in a way that was not humanly possible for me to have caused to a heavy, twenty-foot wooden pew simply by leaning on it as I prayed.

In the corner of my eye, I saw the minister coming toward me, and the only thing that he said was, "Receive what you have been praying for," then he very lightly touched me on the forehead.

Now, before I tell you what happened next, let me tell you what didn't happen. I have been to more than a few church meetings in my life where some minister has been determined to push people over using their own physical force and then claim that it was God—and I want no part of that. This was different.

The man barely touched me, and suddenly there was a bright light and a loud noise, almost like an electrical discharge, only it didn't hurt me at all. It was magnificent. Both of my feet left the ground at the same time, and I fell helplessly back onto the pew, lying there unable to move as the love and mercy and peace of God washed over me again and again in wave after wave. I lay there crying while everyone else ignored me and the service simply went on.

Have Repentance and Salvation Occurred?

Eventually I managed to pull myself together and enjoy the rest of the service, but after that, everything else seemed anticlimactic, more normal and believable. By the time I arrived back at my father-in-law's place, the doctors (at his own request) had basically sent him home to die among his family, but he was still in great pain. First, I told him about all the things that I had seen and the things that had happened to me, and then I laid my hands on his stomach and prayed for him.

I have seen stranger things since that time, but what followed next was really weird and creepy for someone like myself who had never experienced these things before. There was visible movement within my father-in-law's stomach—like the movement that you might see within the belly of a pregnant woman when the baby kicks or moves against her stomach—and this continued for several minutes while I was praying. Then it stopped, and my father-in-law said immediately that the terrible pain that he had been experiencing was completely gone.

No, God did not heal my father-in-law of cancer that day. I don't know why. Perhaps it was his time to go home to be with the Lord. But what I do know is that God had mercy on him and took his pain away. Right to the end, he said that he had no more pain, and to me that was a miracle. God does not always answer prayer in the way that we think He will or in the way that we want Him to, but I still believe that He sometimes answers the sincere and fervent prayers of people, even when their lives are still messed up and they are not yet where He wants them to be spiritually.

Does the experience of signs and wonders and miracles save people? Not necessarily. In this case, it encouraged me to continue to seek after God, but it didn't save me. I still returned to my wicked ways, as do many other people, and that unrepentance would cost me greatly later on in my life. I implore you not to focus on looking for signs and wonders before you repent and obey God. Jesus had this to say about those who want to see signs and wonders before they will believe in Him:

> *Then some of the Pharisees and teachers of the law said to him, "Teacher, we want to see a sign from you." He answered, "A wicked and adulterous generation asks for a sign! But none will be given it except the sign of the prophet Jonah"* (Matthew 12:38–39 NIV).

The truth is that the life and the three-and-a-half-year ministry of Jesus were absolutely overflowing with signs and wonders and miracles. The Word of God tells us that all the wonderful things that He did would have filled volumes if it had all been recorded, but still the wicked demanded to see more before they would believe. They even wanted to put Him to death for healing people on the Sabbath Day. At that point Jesus said that the only sign He would give them was that after they had put Him to death, He would rise on the third day.

Yet even that was not enough of a miracle for some. Many still many refused to believe even after Christ's resurrection had taken place. So, obviously, seeing signs and wonders is no guarantee of salvation, but that does not mean that signs and wonders have ceased, or that they have no value in our modern society. For one thing, signs and wonders show that God is still a God of love, compassion, and mercy—even to sinners. He still wants to heal and deliver us. He still wants to use miracles to get our attention, so that we will listen to His call to us to repent and believe in Jesus Christ for salvation.

18

Signs, Wonders, and Gifts

Signs and Wonders Do Not Save Us

Listen to me: Don't focus on signs and wonders, thinking that if you have seen or experienced healings or deliverances or miracles, that means that you are automatically going to heaven even if you are continuing to walk in deliberate wickedness. Jesus warned the healed persons to "go and sin no more," lest a worse thing come upon them.

Jesus warned those who were delivered from demons to repent, lest the demons return and bring even more wicked ones with them. Jesus Himself marveled that unbelief and disobedience were so deeply entrenched in the lives of many people that they had trouble believing God's Word without seeing signs to confirm it:

> *There was a government official in nearby Capernaum whose son was very sick. When he heard that Jesus had come from Judea to Galilee, he went and begged Jesus to come to Capernaum to heal his son, who was about to die. Jesus asked, "Will you never believe in me unless you see miraculous signs and wonders?" The official pleaded, "Lord, please come now before my little boy dies." Then Jesus told him, "Go back home. Your son will live!" And the man believed what*

> *Jesus said and started home. While the man was on his way, some of his servants met him with the news that his son was alive and well. He asked them when the boy had begun to get better, and they replied, "Yesterday afternoon at one o'clock his fever suddenly disappeared!" Then the father realized that that was the very time Jesus had told him, "Your son will live." And he and his entire household believed in Jesus* (John 4:46–53 NLT).

The point to be made in this passage of Scripture is that this man was not a true believer at first. He came to Jesus in desperation because his son was dying. Then, through the healing of his son, he and the rest of his entire household became true believers in Jesus.

The miracles and gifts of God have two basic purposes: First, they are evidence of God's love and compassion toward us. Second, the Lord desires them to be used to help build up our faith to believe God's message of salvation, which is: "Repent and believe on the Lord Jesus Christ."

Jesus explained to the evil religious leaders of His day that all the church attendance and religious rituals and signs and wonders in the world cannot save us. They only serve to point us toward Jesus. The Holy Spirit's ministry and gifts are dedicated to drawing us toward believing in and being obedient to Christ. If we then choose to reject Christ's call to repent and believe in what He has to say, there can be no more excuse for those who reject the message of the Son of God.

And He Gave Them Power

I have used the NLT version of Mark 6 here for ease of reading, but where the NLT uses the word "authority," the King

James Version uses the phrase "gave them power" in a battle sense. The Greek word used here refers to "knocking and beating up an opponent," so Jesus not only gave them authority over evil spirits, but He gave them a real spiritual ability to do battle with these spirits in the spiritual realm and beat them into submission. If you think that this means that everyone who has the faith to minister in the power of God is automatically saved, do not forget that the traitor, Judas Iscariot, was ministering in power right alongside the other eleven, and look how he ended up.

> *And he was amazed at their unbelief. Then Jesus went from village to village, teaching the people. And he called his twelve disciples together and began sending them out two by two, giving them authority to cast out evil spirits...So the disciples went out, telling everyone they met to repent of their sins and turn to God. And they cast out many demons and healed many sick people, anointing them with olive oil* (Mark 6:6–13 NLT).

In chapter 9 of the gospel of Luke, there is a parallel account of Jesus sending out His twelve disciples, and in this passage, the word power is translated from the Greek word *dunamis*, meaning "miraculous mighty power." Fittingly, dunamis is the root origin of our modern words dynamic, dynamo, and dynamite. This is the same word that Jesus used when He explained to His disciples that even though He would be leaving them, the Father God would send the Holy Spirit to help them:

> *He commanded them, "Do not leave Jerusalem until the Father sends you the gift he promised, as I told you before. John baptized with water, but in just a few days you will be baptized with the Holy Spirit.... You will receive* ***power*** *when the Holy Spirit comes upon you. And you will be my witnesses, telling people about me everywhere—in Jerusalem, throughout Judea, in Samaria, and to the ends of the earth"* (Acts1:4–8 NLT, emphasis mine).

To Build Our Faith and Help Us to Believe

The truth is that, by and large, the human race is a faithless and unbelieving species. Jesus Himself rebuked His own disciples for doubting the Word of God and the testimony of those who declared that He was risen from the dead. For many of His own disciples, they simply would not believe He had risen until Jesus performed the miracle of teleporting and materializing right in their midst behind locked doors. Until they saw Jesus themselves and talked with Him and touched Him, even many of His own disciples would not believe the testimony of others who were declaring that Jesus had risen from the dead:

> *On the evening of that first day of the week, when the disciples were together, with the doors locked for fear of the Jewish leaders, Jesus came and stood among them and said, "Peace be with you!" After he said this, he showed them his hands and side. The disciples were overjoyed when they saw the Lord. Again Jesus said, "Peace be with you! As the Father has sent me, I am sending you." And with that he breathed on them and said, "Receive the Holy Spirit... Now Thomas (also known as Didymus), one of the Twelve, was not with the disciples when Jesus came. So the other disciples told him,*

"We have seen the Lord!" But he said to them, "Unless I see the nail marks in his hands and put my finger where the nails were, and put my hand into his side, I will not believe." A week later his disciples were in the house again, and Thomas was with them. Though the doors were locked, Jesus came and stood among them and said, "Peace be with you!" Then he said to Thomas, "Put your finger here; see my hands. Reach out your hand and put it into my side. Stop doubting and believe." Thomas said to him, "My Lord and my God!" Then Jesus told him, "Because you have seen me, you have believed; blessed are those who have not seen and yet have believed" (John 20:19–29 NIV).

He rebuked them for their lack of faith and their stubborn refusal to believe those who had seen him after he had risen. He said to them, "Go into all the world and preach the gospel to all creation. Whoever believes and is baptized will be saved, but whoever does not believe will be condemned...." After the Lord Jesus had spoken to them, he was taken up into heaven and he sat at the right hand of God.... Then the disciples went out and preached everywhere, and the Lord worked with them and confirmed his word by the signs that accompanied it (Mark 16:14–20 NIV).

Signs and Wonders Are Still Needed

It is a sad thing when those who profess to be Christian leaders have so little compassion for their fellow man that they claim that the miraculous gifts of the Holy Spirit have passed away and they are no longer needed today.

Look around you! The precious gifts of God are needed just as much today as they were needed in the first century A.D.

Such statements are almost as heartless as trying to use the Scriptures to blame those who are sick and oppressed when they don't get well after being prayed for. To make themselves look good, Christian leaders sometimes place further despair and condemnation upon those oppressed of Satan by suggesting that the victims did not have "enough faith" to get healed. Those who think this way will often quote Matthew or Mark to support what they teach.

> *And he did not do many miracles there because of their lack of faith* (Matthew 13:58 NIV).

> *And he could there do no mighty work, save that he laid his hands upon a few sick folk, and healed them. And he marveled because of their unbelief...* (Mark 6:5–6 KJV).

We see here that in Matthew it says that Jesus did not do many miracles, and in Mark it says that He could not do any mighty work. In both cases, it says that the reason was "because of their unbelief." The argument is then given by some people that if Jesus Himself was not able to heal people when they did not have enough faith, how could we ever be successful?

This is what happens when people take the Scriptures out of context and try to use them to justify what they have chosen to believe regardless of whether or not it is what the Bible actually teaches. Sometimes our faith can influence God to move on our behalf, but Jesus Christ does not need our faith in order to perform miracles. Neither is He hindered from performing miracles if our faith is weak.

Even though Jesus remarked about the lack of faith in His own disciples, He still healed those who were brought to Him.

When the father of the demon-possessed child came to Jesus, admitting his own lack of faith and asking for help, Jesus healed and delivered the boy.

And when the demon-possessed man came running out of the tombs, there was no faith involved on the part of the victim. There was only compassion on Christ's part to see that the man needed to be set free from the demons that were tormenting him. The same thing occurred at the pool of Bethesda. The crippled man did not come to Jesus in faith. Jesus came to him and healed him out of love, warning him to go and sin no more lest some worse thing should come upon him.

What about those whom Jesus raised from the dead? Dead people have no faith to be able to respond to Jesus. They have no faith at all left to respond in this life. They are dead. Yet Jesus still had the power to raise them up. No, the true meaning of Matthew 13 and Mark 6 can only be obtained when we look at the portions of Scripture that have been deliberately left out by those who are in error.

Difference Between What God Is Unable to Do and What God Cannot or Will Not Do

God is omnipotent. God is able do anything He wants to do. He does not require one iota of our human faith in order to perform signs and wonders. Therefore, when these passages talk about Jesus not "being able" to perform many signs and wonders in His hometown, we should be looking for another explanation other than Christ's own ability, and the answer we are looking for is included in the very same passages of Scripture.

In order to understand the true meaning of these passages, it is important to know the settings in which they occur. Jesus had been traveling for some time performing signs and wonders all throughout the land of Israel, and then He returned to His hometown, where His own people rejected Him as the Messiah. They become offended at Jesus, rather than believing in Him. The key Scripture portion in both of these passages is that the people became "offended" in Jesus:

And they were offended in him... (Matthew 13:57 KJV).

And they were offended at him (Mark 6:3 KJV).

Hopefully, you are beginning to see that these Scriptures have nothing to do with Christ's actual ability to perform signs and wonders. They are talking about the fact that Jesus Christ will not override the free will of those who choose to reject Him. The kind of unbelief and the kind of offense being talked about here was the deliberate rejection of Jesus Himself.

Jesus will not force Himself upon anyone who refuses to believe in Him and His ministry. The reason that not many miracles were performed in Jesus' hometown was that they did not want to believe in Him. They chose to personally reject Jesus as the Messiah. Therefore, in that situation, Jesus could not and would not override their free will because God is a God of love and freedom, not force and compulsion.

God Acts Even When Our Faith Is Lacking

Aside from the aforementioned experience with my trip to the United States and praying for my father-in-law, the only exposure that I had ever had regarding the signs and wonders of God was what I had seen on TV. There was really no way to verify how much (if any) of it was real, and how much was a product of hype, hysteria, and hucksterism.

For years, I had listened to local preachers who taught that the time of signs and wonders and miracles and the gifts of the Holy Spirit were over. However, as more and more local ministers and TV preachers in the world have begun to research the Scriptures and have started to disagree with those who refuse to believe the Word of God, things are beginning to change in the churches of today.

More and more signs and wonders are starting to manifest in the lives of those who choose to have faith in God's Word. God loves to respond to our faith. I have found that when we step out in even the smallest amount of faith to believe God's Word and act on it, God then steps up to confirm to us that His Word is true. Believing in Jesus gives Him permission to act even when our own faith is lacking.

19

A God of Miracles

The Door for Miracles and Wonders to Occur

Up until the time that I fully committed my heart to live for Jesus in 1981, I had almost no experience in seeing God moving in signs and wonders. I had previously only been in contact with people who did not really believe that God still moves in this way in our generation.

I also knew from my personal history that I had virtually no power in my life to overcome my own addictions and resist my own urges to sin. I knew that I needed something from God to help me overcome my own wicked nature if the rest of my life was going to be different from the ways that had brought me to destruction and so close to death.

I realized that I needed the power of the Holy Spirit in my life if I was going to overcome my sin, so I told God that I wanted it all—everything that God had made available for me to use, including the phenomenon of speaking in tongues. I was through doubting God and holding back through unbelief. I invited the Holy Spirit into my life, not just to be there, but to give me the power I needed over the areas where I had tried and failed to serve God for many years.

Then, gradually, as I learned to trust God and trust the Holy Spirit's guidance, things started to happen in my life and in the lives of those around me. God began to prove to me that He is the same yesterday, today, and forever. He still performs miracles today.

Faith Comes by Hearing

I have been a Christian leader now for well over thirty years, and I still do not see supernatural signs and wonders occur every day in my life. Yet that does not mean that I have never seen God do the miraculous. Over the years, I have seen God move sovereignly in many different ways, so I have felt that it would be an encouragement to you, the reader, for me to include some of these testimonies in this chapter to help build your faith to believe that God is still a God of the miraculous and that we never know when He will prove it to us.

One thing that I have learned over the years is that there is a correlation between how much we see regarding God's power and God's gifts and whom we decide to associate with. When I spent little time with God and doubted God myself, and I was surrounded by people who doubted God, there were no signs and wonders. Then, when I chose to start praying more and believing and obeying God and associated with people who still believed that God still worked in wondrous ways, I began to experience the power of God in my life on many occasions. One of the reasons that God encourages us not to forsake gathering together with other people is that being around other people of faith and hearing their testimonies help to increase our own faith in God and in what God can do. Then we will begin to see the miraculous take place in our own lives.

Delivered by God from Addiction

That was my prayer to God on that night when I turned my life over to Jesus in 1981. I had tried unsuccessfully, over and over for years, to be set free from my addictions, but all that time I had not really been trusting God. That night, God made a promise to me that if I repented, if I made the choice to start believing God and obeying Him, then Jesus would set me free from the chains that Satan had bound me with ever since I had been introduced to the lure of pornography, alcohol, and drugs as a young child.

God promised me that He would help me overcome these things and the evil spirits behind them. He would give me victory over all of the power of Satan and his temptations, as long as I was willing to continue to listen to the Word of God and walk in obedience.

Over the years, God has remained faithful to His promise. Furthermore, I have seen God do the same thing over and over again for many different people, and it doesn't matter what kind of addiction it is. If people are totally committed to repentance, to believe and obey the Lord, God always keeps His end of the bargain.

My own mother was a good example of this. Mom accepted Jesus and received the Holy Spirit when she was in her sixties, and God delivered her from a lifelong struggle with depression and a lifelong addiction to cigarettes and alcohol. She lived the remainder of her life as a joyful, solid, dedicated Christian.

I have come in contact with many other people who testify of God delivering them from addictions of all kinds, prescription and hard drug addictions, sexual addictions, self-harm addictions, violent addictions, even TV and video game addictions. In every case, God has proven that His Word is still true—yesterday, today, and forever. You might not classify deliverance from addictions as a miracle, but I do. Deep in my heart, I know that if God had not intervened, I would still be a prisoner of my sin to this very day.

Have you managed to escape addiction on your own? If so, then good for you, but even that will not save you. God has something even more valuable for us than becoming addiction-free. God's Word tells us that the world is already condemned, but if we repent of our sins and accept Jesus Christ as our Savior, then heaven is our reward and the earth is our inheritance. Why not add salvation to the victory you have achieved over your addictions?

If you still need to hear of miracles happening today in order to believe that salvation through Jesus Christ is real and that God still performs wonders, here are just a few that I have experienced in my own life. I hope that my testimony to you about them will help to build your faith to believe that God does love us and wants us to know that, if we pray to Him in faith, He still wants to move in signs and wonders today.

A Miracle of Teleportation in My Life

There are several recorded instances of God performing miracles of teleportation in the Bible. In John 6, we read of the disciples who were in the midst of a lake when a terrible storm arose and their boat was in danger of sinking. At that point Jesus came to them, walking on the water, and the moment that He stepped into the boat, the entire boat was immediately teleported to safety on the other side of the lake.

Then there is the record after Christ's resurrection when the disciples were all meeting behind locked doors for fear of the Jews, and Jesus teleported Himself inside the locked room.

Lastly, we have the scriptural testimony of the time when the apostle Philip was ministering to the Ethiopian eunuch in the middle of the desert, and after the man accepted Christ, Philip suddenly vanished and found himself in the next town. I guess that God just decided to bless Philip by sparing him the long trek through the desert to his next destination.

As fascinating as I found these stories to be, I had never imagined that anything like that would ever happen to me—and yet it did. I was in my Datsun pickup on my way home from the next town. It was nighttime, and I had just started into a notoriously sharp S curve known as Hagman's Corner, named after the farmer who owned the surrounding land. Then I saw something that scared the wits out of me. There, framed in my headlights, were three full-grown cows.

One cow was standing on my side of the road, one was straddling the middle line, and one was in the opposite lane. There was no time to stop, no way to drive between them, and driving off the shoulder was out of the question because there was a deep gulley that led down to a creek on both sides of the road. It would have meant a horrendous crash and possible death if I had tried to take that route of escape.

There was no way out. I gripped the steering wheel as hard as I could and closed my eyes tightly to protect them from any flying glass. Then I braced myself for the massive impact that I was sure was going to occur from hitting a thousand-pound cow at sixty miles an hour. At the same time, I shouted one word at the top of my lungs: "JESUS!"

It only took a second or two to realize that something miraculous had happened because there was no impact! I thought that maybe God had moved one of the cows out of the way, so I looked in the rearview mirror and saw that they were all still completely blocking the road—behind me. It was then that I realized that God had not moved the cows—He had teleported me, truck and all, from one side of the cows to the other side of the cows. Thank You, Jesus! I have never experienced anything quite like that since then, but I am grateful that God heard my prayer on that day.

God Knows How to Find Things

There are three instances that particularly stand out in my memory when God directed me to find something. The first was when we were conducting an open-air church service and concert in the ballfield of a small town north of where I live. One of the ladies in the worship team was upset that she had lost her glasses somewhere that day, and she had no idea when or where she had lost them. As she could hardly see a thing without them, I encouraged the group that we should all pray for the Lord's help to find the lady's glasses.

Immediately after the prayer I felt led of the Lord to walk all the way through the outfield and into the knee-high grass. At a certain point, I stopped and looked down, and you guessed it, there were the glasses. There was no way that we would have ever found those glasses on our own. I know that it was God who helped me find them.

On another occasion, we were upstairs praying in our church when some brazen thief walked into the sanctuary and stole the guitar and amplifier of the president of the Bible college who happened to be on the praise and worship team that day. Of course, the first thing that we did was to pray for the Lord to help us get the equipment back.

Now, I live in a city with a population of over a hundred thousand people. There are over a dozen pawnshops in the city, but after our prayer I told the group that I believed that the Lord was leading me to go to a particular pawnshop, so they said that I should go. I got in my truck, drove to the shop, found the very distinctive guitar and amp sitting there, paid the pawnshop owner the twenty dollars that it had cost him for the items, and brought them back with me to return them again to their very happy owner.

God Knows How to Find People

The third situation involved finding a particular person during a missionary trip to Guatemala. Before I left Canada, one of my pastors had told me of a certain missionary who was doing a good work down in Guatemala. They asked me to try to contact him while I was down there in order to see if there was some way that we could help him, and I was given a sum of money to distribute wherever I felt the Holy Spirit was leading me to donate it while I was in Guatemala.

There were a lot of answers to prayer surrounding that trip to Guatemala, but this one example shows how God can not only find people, but that He has great timing, as well. After arriving in Guatemala, I actually managed to reach the man's home by phone, but the person answering the phone did not speak English. I only knew enough Spanish to glean from the conversation that the man was ministering somewhere up in the mountains and that they would not be able to reach him until he returned.

I was convinced that the Lord wanted me to meet with this man, so I made the two-hundred-kilometer bus ride from Guatemala City to the man's home city of Quetzaltenango, trusting in faith that the Lord would make a way for me to find the minister. Upon arriving in Quetzaltenango, I went to the

Canadian consulate and learned that they did know of the man, but they did not know where his office was or how to contact him. I was out of ideas, so I turned to prayer.

Many Central American cities have large town squares with monuments and a park area in the center, so I left the consulate and started walking around the perimeter of the town square, praying to God, letting Him know that if He wanted me to get in contact with this man, I was out of options and He was going to have to make it happen Himself.

I continued praying as I walked around the square, and I was almost back to where I had started, when I looked down a side street and saw a sign identifying a Spanish/English school, and so I went inside. If nothing else, I thought, at least someone there would speak English and maybe they would be able to help me. "Oh, yes," they said when I asked about the man. "We know him. His office is right across the street"—and the man pointed to a building on the other side of the street with a tiny sign on the door. Just as he was saying this, a pickup truck pulled up to the door and someone went inside. I thanked the man at the school and rushed over to talk to whoever had just arrived.

This was the man I had been looking for! He had only driven back down to the office to get something that he needed, and he was headed back out, miles into the mountains, right away. Ten minutes earlier or ten minutes later, and I would have missed him. This was no coincidence. If I had not walked around the town square praying, and if I had not gone into the school at the exact time that I did, this man would have come and gone and I would have never found him, but God knows how to arrange divine appointments.

I accepted the missionary's invitation to accompany him

back up into the mountains to see the work that they were doing there. He explained to me that they had felt the Lord's leading to raise up a building in a rural village that would serve as a multipurpose community hall, a source of clean water and a place of worship. It would be a place where people could come for clean, safe water to use for drinking, and there would be an outdoor laundry area with concrete tables and sinks where people could wash their clothes. Inside, they could hold meetings and church services.

His ministry had proceeded with the project on faith, trusting that God would provide for their needs as they arose. The well and pump had been installed, and the water was flowing. The lumber for the walls and the material for the roof were all purchased and sitting there ready to be installed, but that was as far as they had been able to go. There were no more immediate funds to purchase the concrete that was necessary to complete the floor of the building and the washing and drinking areas.

When I asked him how much this would cost and then informed him that the Lord had provided me with the funds to help them complete the building, they were most grateful. That evening, dozens of villagers came from miles around to participate in a beautiful worship service on the building site, and the next day I said my good-byes and headed back to Guatemala City to see what other adventures the Lord would have for me next. I'll tell you a little more about those later on in this book.

God Still Heals Today

I can't tell you why God does not heal everyone who comes to Him in prayer. I can't even tell you why I don't get healed every time I ask for prayer, but I can tell you that God has healed me at various times during my life, and I have also seen and heard testimonies of God healing numerous others, even in the small church of less than fifty people that I attended back in the early 1980s.

One of the ladies there told of how the doctors had diagnosed her with a tipped womb and had informed her that the child she was soon about to bear would definitely have to be delivered by Caesarian section. The whole church had prayed that God would heal this condition, and after about four hours of labor, out popped a healthy baby.

Another pregnant woman had managed to get herself crushed between a truck and a cement wall because the truck had been left running and her toddler had slipped it into gear as she was walking by. This time the doctors told her that her several internal injuries and the injuries to the baby were severe, and the baby could be born abnormal or even die during childbirth. Again the church prayed, and again a perfectly healthy baby boy was born when the time was right.

There was also the time when I went to pick my mother up for church and found her half-dressed and crying because she wanted to go to church but her arthritis had become so bad that she was not even able to zip up her dress. I helped her finish dressing and encouraged her to go to church and then go forward to have her arthritis prayed for. It was a wonderful service, and when Pastor Claudia invited people to come forward for prayer after the service, Mom went to the front. The pastor and the entire church gathered around Mom and started praying for her until she collapsed and hit the floor so hard that I was concerned she might have hurt herself, but no, that was not the case.

Mom came back up bouncing and jumping around and

praising God like an eight-year-old, and she never suffered from arthritis again for the rest of her life. Right up to the time of her death, she remained flexible enough to put one hand behind her head and one behind her back and touch her fingers together. I certainly can't do that myself, and I am sure that most of you can't either.

A Personal Tragedy Became a Testimony of Healing

A few things that I have learned about God over the years is that He does not always do things in the same way as He has done them before. In fact, I believe that Jesus deliberately healed people in many different ways to demonstrate to us that there is no particular formula or technique that can be used to make healing happen. Our job is simply to ask for God's help and not give up, even if the answer doesn't come right away, or even if it doesn't come the way we expect it to.

Let me give you a few examples from my own life. About three years after I was saved, through a moment of ignorance and carelessness I received second-degree burns to my hands and right leg and third-degree burns to my left calf and the back of my knee. As a matter of fact, when the accident happened, there was not even any water around to put out the fire. If it had not been for the selfless act of an unsaved friend who fell on the flames with his own body and smothered them, I could have died that day or at least have been severely crippled for the rest of my life.

As it was, I ended up in the hospital with second- and third-degree burns. I had to endure the agony of having the dead skin removed and weeks of rehab in the hospital before they sent me home, unable to use my left leg at all. After keeping an eye on it for a while, my doctor finally informed me one Monday morning that the leg was not healing. Without skin grafts, it did not look like I was going to regain any use of the leg—and I could even lose the leg altogether. Now, I don't know how much you know about skin grafts, but in those days they used to cut a piece off your backside and then use it to try to grow new skin on your leg—not at all a pleasant experience to look forward to.

I didn't want to be crippled for the rest of my life, but I did not like the idea of going through that process either, so I called Pastor Claudia and asked if she and the rest of the prayer team would please pray for God to heal my leg. She said that they would do that, and I thought that would be the end of it.

Then, about a half hour later, there was a knock on the door. When Mom answered the door, in came about a half-dozen ladies and an accordion. They had all driven twenty miles together to come and anoint me with oil and pray for me in person.

First, we all had an impromptu praise and worship session that was quite beautiful. Then they anointed me with oil, laid hands on me, and began praying. I felt the power of God begin to flow through my body. I'm telling you that these women were real prayer warriors. They knew how to pray. By the time they had left my house, I was sure that God had touched me.

The next day, I had another appointment with my doctor. I went in with high spirits, but my hopes were crushed when he told me that there was no change in the condition of my leg and he was going to book me into the hospital the next day for the skin grafts. What a letdown.

The day after that, I hobbled to my car on crutches and drove fifty miles to the closest burn center, where they put me on a gurney, stuck an IV needle into my arm, and wheeled me into the operating room. When the doctor unwrapped the bandages from my leg to prepare it for surgery and saw my leg, he remarked that he didn't really understand it, but the leg was now healing well and they would not have to perform the skin graft. They pulled out the IV, rewrapped my leg, and sent me home! I was on the road to recovery. Thank You, Jesus!

Sometimes God Heals in Stages

It's true. My burned leg was an excellent example of this. Hebrews 11:1 tells us that faith is the substance of things hoped for and the evidence of things unseen. God wants us to continue to have faith in Him, even when we don't see any immediate results. The interesting thing is that God performed my healing in two stages. The first stage was when the doctors told me that it was starting to heal and I would not need skin grafts.

But after I got home, my own doctor informed me that even though my leg was starting to heal, it was still going to be a long and painful rehabilitation process that would require daily applications of ointment and keeping the leg completely wrapped in burn dressings and bandages for a period of up to a year or two before the healing process was complete.

I tried a few times to exercise faith that God would immediately complete the healing process, but each time I tried removing the bandages for any extended period of time, the skin on my leg would dry up and crack and bleed, until I had to give in and reapply the ointment and bandages. I was grateful to God for sparing me from the skin grafts, but in the back of my mind I was thinking that God was now allowing me to go through this long trial because of the sinful life that I had once led.

In my mind I cited my past sins as the reason for God not

completely healing me now. I had gone from being a sinner to carrying a bit of a martyr complex. I was ready to suffer for another two years if that was what God wanted of me, but God had something else in mind—something much better.

The accident had actually happened about two months before I started Bible college, and I now firmly believe that this was an attack of Satan designed to keep me out of the ministry, but it didn't work. I was still on crutches when the first semester of Bible college started, but I made it there. A short time into my first year, the Lord arranged for another divine appointment that would teach me some humility through someone whom I needed to listen to if I wanted to be healed completely.

A Lesson About Humility and Judging Others

Not long after I started Bible college, we were told that we would be having a guest speaker that week and the name sounded familiar to me. Once the person showed up, I recognized him as the man who had wired the trailer that I was living in with such incompetence that you had to go outside on the front porch to turn the living room light off when you went to bed at night. This was really annoying when it was raining or cold and snowing outside.

My first reaction was, What could this person possibly have to say that would be of any value? Immediately, the Lord stopped me in my tracks, reminding me that I had made many mistakes in my own life and that He was still using me. God told me that this man was a chosen vessel and what he had to say was important for me to learn. "Listen to him."

It turned out that the bulk of the man's message was that God's love toward us and His desire to heal and deliver us is unconditional. God's desire for us to be whole has no bearing whatsoever on our past sins. It was like God was using this man as a guiding light for me to help me change my way of thinking. I began to realize that God did not want me to suffer for another two years. God really wanted to heal me completely. It was like a switch had been turned on, and I instantly knew that I was healed.

I went home that night and thanked God for His healing touch. Then I took the bandages off and fell into a deep sleep. When I woke up in the morning, my skin was soft and healed, and I have never had trouble with my leg since that time. I still have the visible scars from the accident, but the skin is still soft and my leg still works fine thirty years later.

A footnote to this story is that God taught me something useful that day about vanity and about judging others. When the preacher asked the next day if anyone wanted prayer for healing, the Lord put it in my heart to testify before everyone there of what God had done for me as a result of this man's message, and I was able to encourage others to believe, as well. Then I went up for prayer with everyone else to demonstrate to God that I was willing to listen to Him regardless of the vessel He had chosen to use to speak to me.

The truth be known, God will even speak to us through unsaved people at times. If we are wise, we will learn to set our pride aside, humble ourselves, and listen to the Word of God regardless of the source, even if it is from an unbeliever, even if it is from some drunk or drug addict lying in a gutter. The wise person will listen for God's Word, whatever the source. I am not suggesting that you believe everything that every preacher says. Be sure to compare what they say with what God has to say in His Word, and then eat the meat and spit out the bones.

Never Give Up Praying

It doesn't matter if you are praying for guidance or finances or healing or salvation of your friends or relatives—don't stop. Don't give up. I have seen God heal people instantly. I have seen God heal people in stages, and in one case in my life, I had to keep praying for years before anything happened. In spite of all the other blessings that I had enjoyed from God since 1981, there was one area of my body that the devil did not want to let go of, and that was the bottoms of my feet.

In the early 1970s I had come in contact with a plantar virus. As a result of this, over the years I had developed plantar warts on my heels that had grown to the size of silver dollars and were very deep. There were numerous other smaller ones spread over the bottoms of my feet, as well, but it was the large ones that were the real problem. I don't know how much you know about plantar warts, but when they get that big and run that deep, they hurt you when you walk.

Over the years, I had tried every medical treatment available. First, they tried to remove them surgically. They came back bigger. Then they tried to use liquid nitrogen to kill them by freezing them. My feet hurt so badly after the surgery and the liquid nitrogen that the cures seemed worse than having the warts themselves, and still they came back—bigger than ever.

The final thing that the doctors tried was ultrasound. It wasn't that painful, but it did not work either. The doctors finally gave me the news that with some people, nothing works. They warned me that the warts could just keep getting bigger and more painful and that eventually I might not be able to walk anymore.

Well, maybe the doctors couldn't cure this, but I knew that God could. I kept praying for years for God to heal me, and I kept asking other believers to pray that God would get rid of the warts as well. Then one morning I woke up and my feet felt different; the painful discomfort was gone, and when I looked at my feet, all the warts were completely gone. The night before, they had been as big and as bad as ever, and the next morning they were gone and they have never come back again. Thank You, Jesus!

20

Preparing for Ministry

God Knows How to Guide Our Finances

When I repented and turned to God in 1981, it was a 100-percent commitment. I did not know how or when or where, but I knew that I wanted to serve God from that time forth. I was sure that God wanted me to attend Bible college, but before I could do that, I believed that the Lord wanted me to pay off my debts—and I owed over fifteen thousand dollars.

I had never even managed to save a thousand dollars at once in my entire life, so I asked for the Lord's help and wisdom to make it happen. I knew I couldn't do it by myself. I really don't even know how it all came together, but somehow it did. By 1985 the Lord had enabled me to pay off the fifteen thousand dollars that I owed, plus an additional fifteen thousand that had been my ex-wife's portion of our debt. Not only was everything completely paid off, but I had eighteen thousand dollars in cash left over to pay for the expenses of going to Bible college.

Now, forty-eight thousand dollars might not seem like all that much by today's standards, but remember, this was back in the day when you could buy a house in our neighborhood for about that same amount of money, and the average wage was under three dollars an hour. I have no doubt whatsoever that God made this financial miracle happen.

God Opens Doors for Us

The next step was for me to find a Bible college, and not just any Bible college, but the one that God wanted me to attend. This was not a decision that I took lightly. I did some serious research on this, checking out colleges in Kelowna, Vancouver, and even one in San Jose, California. They were all good, but for some reason I believed that the Lord wanted me to go to Kelowna, British Columbia.

This was somewhat baffling to me because the Bible college in Kelowna was fundamentalist in their teachings, and I was definitely more charismatic in my beliefs. Yet when I informed them of my belief that the gifts of the Holy Spirit were still relevant today, they accepted my application anyway. Okay, then. Everything seemed set. I supposed that this was where God wanted me. Theologically, there were colleges in other cities that would have been a better fit for me, but somehow I felt that God wanted me in Kelowna.

Even though Kelowna had close to a zero vacancy rate, my mom had decided that she wanted to move to Kelowna with me, so I said, “Let’s go!” Somehow God worked it out that we were able to find a house for my mother and I to live in. The money I had saved was enough for a down payment, and there would be enough left over for expenses while I attended my first year at the Bible college. With the Lord’s help, I had found a little house to buy that fit our purpose perfectly, and the price was cheap. Five years later, I ended up selling that house for almost double what I had initially paid for it.

The next step was to find a church to attend. Even though I had been accepted at a fundamentalist college, I was certain that the Lord wanted me to attend a church that believed in the baptism and the gifts of the Holy Spirit. I had heard of a church in Kelowna that sounded like it had what I was looking for, so I went in to speak with them.

The secretary directed me to three gentlemen who were talking together in a side area of the office, one of whom was the senior pastor of the church. I explained to him that I believed that God was directing me to attend Bible college in Kelowna and that I was looking for a charismatic church to attend. I told him the important details of my past, holding nothing back. Then I explained to them that I now wanted to serve God for the rest of my life, and I noticed that all three men were smiling. In fact, they seemed rather amused by what I was saying. I was about to find out why.

The pastor told me that I would be welcome to attend his church, and then he introduced me to the other two men—the president and the vice president of a brand-new charismatic Bible college being formed in Kelowna. It was so new that they had not even advertised it yet. I knew right then that this was where God wanted me to be. Things were definitely looking better in my life.

In the World You Will Have Tribulation

I get annoyed when I hear preachers telling people that all you have to do is believe in Jesus and that you'll be healthy, wealthy, and wise for the rest of your life. To hear them talk, serving Jesus will be all wine, roses, lollipops, and rainbows, as long as you tithe to their church and give generously on top of that. No wonder people get so disillusioned with Christianity. Jesus didn't ever say that. In fact, in John 16:33 He tells us that in this world we are going to have tribulation. We will make mistakes that will cause us problems. Bad things will happen during our lives that are not our fault. We will run across people who will mistreat us and dislike us without cause. Becoming a Christian doesn't change any of that. This is still a world troubled by evil.

The Lord has not promised us that our lives as Christians will always be fair or painless. God has healed me of many things over the years, but I still get hurt and sick on occasion and I have to suffer through it. I cracked a rib the other day, and as I am writing this, I know that unless God performs a miracle, I am in for about three or four weeks of pain before it gets better.

I also know that unless Jesus arrives soon, there will come a day in my future when I will be so old that I will get sick and I will not get better. I will die. I am okay with that because I know that the real promise of Christianity is not that this life will be perfect after we accept Jesus.

The promise of Christianity is that when we accept Jesus Christ, He will give us His Holy Spirit to help us deal with any and every obstacle that comes our way in this lifetime. Then, after our resurrection, Jesus has all of eternity to bless us and more than compensate us for the worst things that could ever happen to us this side of heaven.

Sometimes Things Don't Go According to Plan

When I first arrived in Kelowna, I had everything planned out. I would put the down payment on the house. Mom and I would share the cost of the mortgage payment, and I would be able to use the remaining eight thousand dollars in my savings account to take care of my share of the mortgage and my expenses for my first year of Bible college. And then the bank pulled a fast one on me. They told me that because I was not working, they would not okay the mortgage unless I allowed them to put a lien on my savings account. I was not going to be able to touch that money even though it was mine.

I'm telling you, that hurt. It was only a few months until my first semester was to start, and I had to find a job in Kelowna. To make a long story short, I did find a full-time job working in the factory of a Christian businessman until it was time for my classes to start. Furthermore, it turned out that the man liked me so much that when I started Bible college, he handed me the key to the factory and told me that I could come in during any hours I chose and work part-time while I was attending college. Often something that starts out as an annoyance or a hardship can turn out to be a great blessing in the end.

Another example of this came when I wanted to refinance our mortgage. Interest rates were terrible in those days. I was paying 13.5 percent interest on our mortgage. Then the interest rates dropped over the next year to 11 percent, but the bank refused to refinance for us at the lower rate, and they still refused to release the lien on my savings account even though I had dealt with that very same bank since I had been sixteen years old.

I presented my predicament as a prayer request at school, and another Bible school student loaned me the funds that I needed for my second year of tuition. Then I found another bank that I had never dealt with before. They took over the mortgage at the lower rate without requiring any guarantee, so I got my eight thousand dollars back to repay the other student and to help with my costs for my second year. Things might not go the way that we originally planned them to, but in the end, God works all things together for our good.

Bible College—God's Immersion School

I really loved my first year of Bible school. This was a school that was born of the Spirit of God only one year before I started attending it, and it was a powerful influence in the city of Kelowna and throughout the Province of British Columbia. Five days a week, we would all meet for prayer and worship in the mornings and then go to classes for teaching on many aspects of Christian life and ministry.

Most of the teachers were highly anointed men and women of God as were the guest speakers who would come in to teach a class once or twice a week. The guest speakers were usually evangelists or missionaries who were back home between trips, but sometimes they were just mature Christians from the community who were welcome to give their input. It was a school with a real vision for the Lord—at least that's the way it was in the beginning.

There was a huge diversity of students as well, everything from zealous brand-new converts, to ministry candidates, to longtime believers who were interested in expanding their knowledge and walk with God. In addition to classes (for those who were interested), there were also opportunities to minister in music, witnessing, teaching, and evangelism over the weekends locally and at many other cities across the province. I have a decent baritone voice and a good vocal range, so I volunteered to minister in music and was soon invited to be one of the lead singers after joining the music ministry.

One of the good things about Bible college was that it kept me immersed in the things of God during my formative Christian years, and it gave me a good foundation of Christian doctrine and theology that I now can teach to other people. It was in Bible college that I learned that the dominant gifts of the

Holy Spirit in my life were teaching, prophecy, and the discerning of spirits, gifts that would turn out to be both a blessing and a challenge for me as school and life went on.

Spiritual Conflicts

This Bible college was the dream of a godly man who had little credentials and qualifications in the natural but a strong vision from God to raise up a charismatic Bible college in Kelowna, and that is how it all started. It was a vibrant, living, and powerful move of the Holy Spirit, and students were drawn to it from all over the country. There were even a few from other nations.

During the first couple of years, quite a number of these students went on to enter the ministry in many different capacities, and the school was growing rapidly, as much by word-of-mouth reputation as by any other means. In fact, the church that I now attend as an associate pastor over twenty-five years later was planted by one of those very Bible college graduates, but the college itself was not without its problems.

Unfortunately, over time the spirit of vanity managed to gain a foothold in the college. There were a few bad apples in the bunch—leaders who had the education and the credentials but who did not understand or want the Holy Spirit's ministry in signs and wonders in the college. They managed to convince the president of the Bible college that it would be better for the reputation and growth of the college if a greater emphasis was placed on respectability, learning, and knowledge, and less on active ministry in the gifts and the moving of the Holy Spirit.

By the time I arrived in 1985, these people were already trying to undermine the Holy Spirit and working to create a rift between the college and the charismatic church that had originally sponsored the work and provided the facilities for the college to use.

Things Started in the Spirit Cannot Be Finished in the Flesh

One thing about the ministry of the Holy Spirit moving in signs and wonders is that it seriously disturbs the status quo. When the Holy Spirit begins to move in a gathering of people, there is an unseen spiritual battle going on, and things can get noisy, emotional, and messy—but don't confuse a spiritual battle with disorder.

When people are delivered from demons, it's disturbing when these things manifest when they are cast out. When people are healed of ailments that they have been suffering from for years, it's okay for a spiritual uproar of praise and prayer to erupt for a period of time.

We erupt in joyous pandemonium at sports events when someone scores—and we don't even think twice about it. If we can get that excited over some millionaire sinking a ball into a net or shooting a puck into a goal, how much more excited should we be when someone who has been in bondage to Satan for years is set free by the power of God?

During my first year at Bible college, the Holy Spirit had moved mightily through numerous teachers and students, and many of the gifts of the Holy Spirit were manifested to the help of various students and even some of the leaders. As I mentioned before, I myself was physically healed, as were other people.

There were also words of wisdom, knowledge, and prophecy being given under the authority of the college leaders, but by far the most controversial subject was that occasionally during a time of praise and worship or a ministry time of praying for people, a demon would become exposed and manifest itself. The usual solution was for the students and teachers who understood what was happening to gather around the person who was afflicted and pray over him or her until the rotten thing was cast out and the person was set free.

Of course, this is a ministry that Satan is particularly opposed to, because he wants to keep his victims under his control. He does not want people to be set free. Whenever this happened, it had a tendency to upset some of the other students and teachers who didn't understand what was going on or who didn't want it happening at the school.

Perhaps there was a certain amount of fear involved at times, but I believe that more people were just vainly concerned about presenting an image of respectability to the outside world than they were concerned with seeing people healed and delivered from the devil's grip.

Do Not Grieve or Quench the Holy Spirit

In the Word of God, we are warned not to grieve or quench the Holy Spirit. We grieve the Holy Spirit by sinning, and we quench the Holy Spirit by not listening to Him and by trying to shut Him down and live our lives through our own efforts and wisdom. These things are a recipe for disaster, regardless of whether or not it involves a single person or an entire Bible college.

> *Therefore each of you must put off falsehood and speak truthfully to your neighbor, for we are all members of one body. "In your anger do not sin": Do not let the sun go down while*

you are still angry, and do not give the devil a foothold. Anyone who has been stealing must steal no longer, but must work, doing something useful with their own hands, that they may have something to share with those in need. Do not let any unwholesome talk come out of your mouths, but only what is helpful for building others up according to their needs, that it may benefit those who listen. And do not grieve the Holy Spirit of God, with whom you were sealed for the day of redemption. Get rid of all bitterness, rage and anger, brawling and slander, along with every form of malice (Ephesians 4:25–31 NIV).

Do not quench the Spirit. Do not treat prophecies with contempt (1 Thessalonians 5:19–20 NIV).

During the second year of my attendance at the Bible college, I along with other students were discouraged from moving in our gifts as the Holy Spirit led us. As the emphasis was directed away from reliance upon the Holy Spirit and more toward scholasticism only, we could feel the original spiritual life of the place shriveling up and dying. The rift continued to grow between the college and the local fellowship that had been supporting it, and there was talk of moving the college into its own facility in order to expand it and to distance the college from the local church. It was discouraging, but I decided to stick with it until my graduation. But then things got tough.

Obey God Rather Than Men

In chapter 5 of the book of Acts, the Word of God tells us of a time when the spiritual leaders of Israel confronted Peter and the rest of the apostles to remind them that they had been warned not to preach and teach in the name of Jesus—and this was their response:

> *Then they brought the apostles before the high council, where the high priest confronted them. "We gave you strict orders never again to teach in this man's name!" he said. "Instead, you have filled all Jerusalem with your teaching about him, and you want to make us responsible for his death!" But Peter and the apostles replied, "We must obey God rather than any human authority"* (Acts 5:27–29 NLT).

In the Scriptures, we are encouraged to submit ourselves to those who are in authority over us, but there will also come times during our lives when we will come to a crossroads and have to decide whether we are going to obey God or men. It was only two months before my graduation. I had submitted to the authority of the leadership of the college and I had ceased moving in the gifts of the Holy Spirit as they had instructed me to do, praying all the time that God would raise up others to move in the Spirit—but it did not happen. The spiritual life had gone out of the place.

There had been no manifestation at all of the gifts of God in our midst for months, until a charismatic healing evangelist was invited to speak on a certain day during the final class. As he began testifying of all the wonderful things that God was doing overseas and how God was healing people and delivering many people of evil spirits, I started to feel spiritual life come back into the class and into my own bones.

There was a spiritual electricity in the air that we had not experienced in a long, long time. Then, at the end of the message, the evangelist began to pray, and others joined in enthusiastically, until there was a long silence and I clearly heard the voice of God saying, "Prophesy!"

That started me arguing with God, reminding Him that there were only two months left until my graduation and that I could get expelled for doing what He was asking, but still the silence persisted and God again said, "Prophesy!" This time I opened my mouth, and I don't even remember what I said—but I remember that immediately one of the new students fell on his knees before God and confessed that he was involved in sinful practices that were not of God and he begged to be prayed for so that he could be set free.

This set off a chain reaction of several other students also falling to the floor, crying out in the agony of repentance, needing prayer, and then one of them started writhing around on the floor as a demon manifested itself.

Those of us who knew what was going on joined with the visiting evangelist and the president of the Bible college to pray for the young man until the demon was cast out of him, and then we prayed for the others, as well. It was pretty chaotic for a while, but eventually things calmed down, and the president of the college dismissed the class with the promise that the next day he would explain to everyone what had happened.

After the class, I was called aside to face the college dean, the person who had been the most responsible for the quenching of the Holy Spirit in the school. He told me in front of the president of the Bible college that he did not know whether what had just happened was of God or not, but if I wanted to stay at the school, I would have to stand before the class the next day and apologize for not submitting to the school's authority, and if I prophesied again at any time during the rest of the school year, I would be expelled.

I listened for God's guidance for the right response to this man's edict. I did not want to be expelled, but I was in too far to back out now if God wanted me to do what He had asked. "Submit to them," the Lord said, "but give them a message." I looked the dean in the eyes and told him that I would submit to all that he had asked and leave it up to God to judge between me and him. I told him that if what he was doing was right, then God would bless it, but if not, it would all crumble to nothing. He was seething, but nothing more was said, and we parted company on that note.

The rest of the semester went pretty well, without incident, and things remained as spiritually dry as a bone, but I graduated along with the rest of the class, short of one student who ended up in a psych ward and another who later committed suicide. The college moved to a new location on the other side of town for the following year. Sometimes a few of us would audit a class when a guest speaker was there, but it was never the same as it had been in the beginning.

Eventually, my heart sank when I heard that the school had moved to the larger city of Vancouver for bigger and better opportunities. I was saddened but not surprised to hear that a short time later the school had closed. Now it is many years later. The unfortunate state of affairs is that a large proportion of the people who had attended the Bible college throughout the years are not even serving the Lord anymore. This should serve as a warning to others about how much we need the Holy Spirit to help us and guide us if we want to keep serving God.

> *How foolish can you be? After starting your new lives in the Spirit, why are you now trying to become perfect by your own human effort?* (Galatians 3:3 NLT)

God Calls Me to Guatemala

Once Bible college was over, then came the dilemma of what to do next. I have already told you the story about how I was able to find the missionary in Guatemala. Now let me tell you how I got there in the first place. Often missionary/evangelists will have a chance to be the guest speakers at Bible colleges as an opportunity to speak about their missions work in various countries.

One visitor in particular had inspired me to take a month-long trip to Guatemala to see whether I could help some of the Christian workers there in some small way. I was certain that God wanted me to make the trip. For some unknown reason, I knew that I would have to go right away after Bible college—as soon as possible.

I talked to my pastor and he put me in contact with a couple of groups in Guatemala City who offered me a place to stay while I was there and informed me that there was a great deal of need down there for children's clothing and medical supplies, mentioning that eye droppers, vitamins, and aspirin in particular were in short supply. I told them that I would do my best to bring some of those items with me.

I called a travel agent to put a deposit down and book my flight, which would give me about a month to raise the funds and the donated items for the trip. Fortunately, I already had two large steamer trunks that would be perfect for shipping the children's clothing and medical supplies. All God had to do was to help me fill them.

Ask and You Shall Receive

One thing that I have learned over the years is that if we put our faith in God, He will give us favor with people to accomplish His work. As soon as I informed the pastor that the trip had been arranged, the church took up an offering, and over six hundred dollars was raised to be dispersed in Guatemala at my discretion. I went to a local thrift store and informed them of my mission. They gave me permission to take as much children's clothing as I wanted, so I was able to fill one entire steamer trunk with children's clothing at no cost.

Following that, I went to a medical supply center, and they donated several boxes each containing twelve dozen eye droppers and many other valuable medical items, such as thermometers, tongue depressors, and limb braces—all for free. Finally, I went to a local pharmacy, which provided me with a generous supply of aspirin and vitamins for a very nominal fee, well below wholesale. I was ready to go—all except for one small problem. I needed $2,500 to cover my plane ticket and my living costs while I was down there, and that was proving to be a challenge to come up with.

God Meets Our Needs

I had devised a plan that I thought was more than sufficient to cover my own needs for the trip. I decided that I would be willing to give up my camper van, my travel trailer, and a good quality air conditioner that I had on hand. As soon as I booked my flight, I put ads in the newspapers offering all of these items at very low prices to make sure that they all sold. The van alone was worth $2,500, and I was only asking for half of that, so I did not think there would be a problem raising the money. But three weeks later, I had still been unable to sell a single item. There was only a week to go, and I had not paid for my ticket yet. I was getting desperate. Believe me when I say that my prayer time went into high gear.

Then one day I got a phone call. The man on the line was offering me half of what I was asking for the air conditioner, which was actually about a quarter of what it was worth. I decided that selling it that cheaply would not get me much closer to my goal than not selling it at all. I assured the man of the quality of the unit and managed to convince him to come and take a look at it for the price that I was asking.

A short while later, the man arrived and asked if I was a Christian, because he had noticed the JESUS IS LORD bumper sticker on the back of the camper van. That started a conversation about why I was selling the air conditioner and the fact that I was also selling the camper van and the travel trailer to pay for the cost of my mission trip. The man thought about it for a minute, and then remarked that the camper van was reasonably priced and asked to see it. Then he asked to see the trailer, as well.

I had been trying unsuccessfully for weeks to sell these items on my own, and then God brought me one man in one day who listened to my testimony about what I believed God was calling me to do, and in the end he bought everything that I had for the exact amount that I needed to raise to pay my expenses for the trip. God is good!

Then the day came for the trip. I showed up at the airport with a tiny carry-on suitcase for my own belongings and two massive steamer trunks that were way overweight. I explained to the airline employees what I was doing. They passed me through with no extra charges for any overweight luggage, and I was on my way.

God Gives You Favor with Men

When the plane set down in Guatemala City and I headed for customs, I came face-to-face with the reality that I was not in Canada anymore. There were armed guards with rifles and submachine guns everywhere, and they all looked like they were ready to take you down if you so much as got out of line. As I entered the long lineup, I could see that absolutely every bag was being opened and checked, and that made me uneasy, putting me into prayer mode with a furious intensity.

You have to realize how serious this situation was. Normally, it takes months to arrange this type of venture to a third-world country. Permissions from government officials needs to be granted, and people need to be placed in the know about what was happening. I had none of that in place. All I had was a letter from one Christian organization verifying that I was coming to help them and that I would be staying with them.

On top of this, I was entering a nation that was rampant with corruption on many different levels, and I was bringing items into the country that were worth thousands of dollars on the black market. They could have demanded that I pay an exorbitant fee—in other words, a bribe—before they would release anything. It was even possible that everything would be confiscated, I would be refused entry into the country, and there would have been nothing that I could have done about it.

Worse than that, they could have accused me of trying to smuggle contraband into the country, taken everything I had, and then thrown me into jail—and again, there would have been nothing I could have done about it.

I began to pray with great intensity that God would give me favor with these people and that none of these things would happen. When my turn came for my baggage to be examined, I placed my small carry-on bag on the counter first, followed by the trunk with the children's clothing, and the most valuable and controversial trunk, the one with all of the medical supplies in it, went on the counter last.

The customs official dug thoroughly through my small bag, set it aside, and opened the steamer trunk full of children's clothes. As he rifled through all of the clothes, I saw his face turn from normal to angry and he started rapidly shouting at me in Spanish, clearly thinking that I was trying to smuggle these items into the country. This is not good, I thought. If they are this upset about children's clothing, what are they going to do when they get to the medical supplies valued at thousands of dollars? I prayed even harder as I attempted to explain the situation to him.

Then a more senior official was called over. I showed him the letter from the Christian organization indicating that I was coming to help them, and I explained to the official in what little Spanish I knew that the clothes were not going to be sold but given to the orphans and poor children. The man looked me in the eyes for a moment, talked to his underlings, and said one word to me: "Pase," meaning to go ahead, and he waved me toward the exit. Nobody seemed to even notice that the third case had not been opened yet. It was like they didn't even see it sitting there.

I quickly grabbed the unopened case containing the medical supplies and put it on the bottom of my luggage carrier. Nobody said anything. I closed up the trunk with the children's clothing and my carry-on bag and placed them on top. I headed for the door, still praying with all that was within me as I left. As I reached the door, someone coming through saw my white skin and asked, "Are you Michael Hunter from Canada?" It was my contact from the missionary organization. "Yes! Let's go—quickly," I said quietly.

After we got into the car, I filled him and his companions in on everything that had happened, including the officials overlooking the trunk with the medical supplies, and we all praised and thanked God that He had watched over me and the much-needed items. It turned out that the fellow who had picked me up did not even know for sure when I was going to be at the airport. He had just shown up, hoping that I would be there.

God Has Great Timing

On the way back to the missionary compound, I filled my hosts in on some of the items that I had brought with me, and they were ecstatic. That very day, they were scheduled to go on a medical inoculation mission to the surrounding villages, and many of the items that I had brought would be useful in that venture.

When we arrived back at the compound, we found that the bus was all loaded and ready to go, but one of the tires that they had taken in to be fixed was unrepairable. It would have to be replaced, but there was no money for the three hundred plus dollars that would cost. Guess who had been given money for just such an emergency? In a short time they were on their way. Upon reporting back that evening, they testified that many people had been helped medically and over sixty had given their hearts to the Lord.

Soon I was back home in Kelowna again, with a slide presentation and a testimony of all the exciting things that God had done on the trip. God had done many wonderful things for me during the seven years between truly accepting Jesus and the time I returned from my mission trip. Most importantly, I knew that I was born again, a new creature in Christ Jesus, and I was looking forward to whatever God had planned next for me.

After arriving back in Kelowna, I hosted several services in different places to tell of all the good things that God had done, and several people prophesied how God would continue to use me in mighty ways. Some of those prophecies have already come true; others may yet occur; and some may never happen—but one in particular rang true in my spirit and stood out from all the others. The prophet said, "I see you ministering the Word of the Lord to people in a small confined space." I was curious. I wondered what God meant by that.

21

Don't Look at Circumstances

Satan Can Use Old Sins to Attack and Test You

God had blessed me in many ways during the years between 1981 and 1988. I was saved and baptized in the Holy Spirit. I was delivered from financial debt. I had been physically healed from numerous ailments. I had witnessed God move supernaturally many times. I was a new person in Christ Jesus, and I had even changed my first name from Barry to Michael.

My legal name had always been Michael Barry, but for some reason, my parents had always chosen to call me by my middle name, Barry. Then, after I committed to the Lord in 1981, I discovered that the name Barry means "a spear." In a good connotation, one might think of a spear being a warrior's weapon, but in my eyes, I saw my previous life as like the guy who thrust a spear in the side of Jesus on the cross to make sure that He was dead. I made the decision that from that time forward, I would go by my real name, Michael, which means "he who is like the Lord."

Life was good. Then, no later than a week after I returned from Guatemala, I got a phone call from the police, informing me that I was going to be charged for a crime that I had committed before I had ever repented and come to the Lord in 1981. This was something that I had done my best to reconcile and clear up back in 1981, but I had been told at the time that the victims were not pressing charges and that would be the end of it. Now, seven years later, the crown prosecutors had decided that they were going to proceed on their own, due to the seriousness of the charges, citing that they were going to make an example of me as a deterrent to others. God was about to allow my faith to be severely tested.

Problems That We Create Ourselves

Remember this: God will never do evil to you, and neither will God ever tempt you to do evil. However, God will occasionally remove His protection from us and allow Satan to tempt us. Remember, it was Satan, not God, who tempted Adam and Eve in the Garden of Eden, and it was Satan who tempted Christ in the wilderness after His baptism:

> *And remember, when you are being tempted, do not say, "God is tempting me." God is never tempted to do wrong, and he never tempts anyone else. Temptation comes from our own desires, which entice us and drag us away. These desires give birth to sinful actions. And when sin is allowed to grow, it gives birth to death* (James 1:13–15 NLT).

When various trials and tribulations come our way in life, Satan will often try to convince us that God is at fault and that God is doing it to us. He'll try to convince us that God is punishing us for some reason. Remember, that's what he did to Job, and that's what he still does to believers today.

Whenever trials come in life, we must not undermine our own faith by falsely accusing God and asking God, "Why are You doing this to me?" In addition, there will also be times in our lives when we can't even fully blame Satan because what we are suffering now is sometimes a product of our own past sins. In these cases, God expects us to suffer the consequences of our transgressions without complaining and keep serving the Lord, trusting that He will bring good out of the situation in the end.

> *For what glory is it, if, when ye be buffeted for your faults, ye shall take it patiently? But if, when ye do well, and suffer for it, ye take it patiently, this is acceptable with God* (1 Peter 2:20 KJV).

> *And we know that all things work together for good to those who love God, to those who are the called according to His purpose* (Romans 8:28 NKJV).

> *Do not fear any of those things which you are about to suffer. Indeed, the devil is about to throw some of you into prison, that you may be tested, and you will have tribulation ten days. Be faithful until death, and I will give you the crown of life* (Revelation 2:10 NKJV).

Know Who Your Enemy Is

When I was a young man, I used to shake my fist at God and ask Him why He was doing these things to me. Why was all of this happening to me? Then Jesus and the Holy Spirit came into my life, and I finally realized that I am my own worst enemy. I was the one responsible for many of the problems in my life. Furthermore, I now understand that any trials that I am not directly responsible for are caused by an even worse enemy—Satan and those he commands.

It was Satan who tried to take my life in the car crash in

1972. It was Satan who tried to take my life in the fire in 1984, and now, after serving the Lord for seven years, Satan was manipulating the circumstances to try to turn me against God in 1988, but I no longer believed the devil. I believed in God.

All of the thoughts and accusations I had were right there in my head, fighting for dominance: You have served God for seven years and what good did it do? God doesn't care about you! Where is your God now? You're going to prison where you belong, and God won't help you there!

The one thing that Satan had not counted on in all of this was that I was no longer a slave to sin, I no longer believed his lies, and I now trusted that God would be in control no matter what the outcome was. Jesus Christ had truly set me free. The truth was that I was guilty and I knew that I deserved to go to prison for the things that I had done, but I also knew that God was now my Father and I was His son, and I would continue to be free even in prison, if it came to that. I also knew that the only reason God was allowing this to happen after seven years of serving Him was that He had a purpose in it all.

> *Jesus said, "If you hold to my teaching, you are really my disciples. Then you will know the truth, and the truth will set you free…." Jesus replied, "Very truly I tell you, everyone who sins is a slave to sin. Now a slave has no permanent place in the family, but a son belongs to it forever. So if the Son sets you free, you will be free indeed"* (John 8:31–36 NIV).

22

From Pulpit to Prison

I Find You Guilty

The trial was the hardest thing I have gone through. I never tried to deny anything or blame anyone else, but to have to stand publicly before people and state that I was guilty broke my heart all over again. When I uttered the plea of guilty, all of the pain, shame, regret, guilt, and condemnation regarding the person I used to be came rushing back. I broke down on the stand for a few moments, and the judge waited for me to regain my composure.

The prosecution was pushing for the maximum penalty without sending me to federal prison—a sentence of two years less a day. The only thing that I had in my favor was a huge stack of references from pastors, employers, landlords, friends, and even a parole officer whom I had been working with to help young offenders, all of them testifying that I was a different person now, not the same one who had once been a criminal.

The judge told me that he believed that I was remorseful and unlikely to reoffend. He said he was moved to leniency by the letters that he had read about the changes in my character, but that still did not alter the fact that I was guilty. As a deterrent to others, he was sentencing me to eight months in prison to begin immediately. Once the sentence was handed down, I was not even discouraged. I was actually relieved. The stress of not knowing what was going to happen was finally gone. It was like a huge burden had been lifted from my shoulders, and I trusted that if I was going to go to prison, it was because God wanted me there for some reason.

I was taken directly from the courtroom to the sheriff's van and had to face the added humiliation of being driven to prison by a female sheriff who knew me. I had even once had a crush on her in high school. But instead of letting it get me down, I turned the five-hour van ride into an opportunity to admit my guilt to her and witness to her of all of the things that God had done since I had given my heart to Him. I have not seen her since, but I know that she was going through some trials of her own, and I believe that some of the things that I said to her touched her heart for Jesus.

Some of You Will Be Cast into Prison

I am not sure what the new facility is like now, but the old Prince George Regional Correctional Facility was certainly no country club prison. It was a formidable place surrounded with high chain-link fences topped with razor wire. When I arrived, all of my belongings except for my Bible were confiscated and stored. New prisoners were given an orange shirt and pants, a pair of underwear, and a pair of slippers, and then we were all ushered into a room and ordered to strip off our street clothing to ensure that no one was hiding anything in any opening in our bodies. Then we were taken to our cells.

I was pulled aside by the warden and told that I was scheduled for the maximum-security wing, but due to overcrowding, he had looked at my file and asked if I was willing to be put into the general population wing. This was a facility built for 150 inmates, and at the time there was about double that many who were incarcerated there. Almost every cell had double occupancy. I told him that I would be willing to do whatever he wanted and that I was going to do my best to stay out of trouble. I only asked that I would have the option of moving to the maximum-security wing at a future date if it looked like there was going to be trouble that I could not avoid. He agreed, and I got my first glimpse of prison life.

The beds in the general population were steel bunks with three-inch mattresses that kept you away from the cold steel but offered little comfort. The biggest culture shock was that there was no privacy anywhere there, not even in the showers or toilets, and the cell doors were left open unless there was a lockdown for some reason. It was certainly a place where you had to be aware of your surroundings at all times and watch your back.

Was I afraid? No, not really. I wasn't careless, but I chose to believe that God had me there for a reason, and I knew that God was well able to protect me even in prison if He chose to do so. I will say, though, that I was prayerful in everything I did and said. I also remained in constant prayer for the Holy Spirit to give me the wisdom and discernment of how to deal with any potential dangers that might arise. I'm telling you, if you want to learn how to pray with sincerity and intensity, prison is one place where you will learn how to do it, although I hope no one reading this book ever has to go there.

Even if Satan himself had put me in prison, I knew that God was going to use it for His good, so my main goal was to discover what it was that God wanted me to do while I was in there, and then make the most that I could out of the situation in which I found myself. I knew that I was at peace about the whole thing. God's Word had reminded me that there was a peace of God that transcends all understanding for those who learn to trust God:

> *Rejoice in the Lord always. I will say it again: Rejoice! Let your gentleness be evident to all. The Lord is near. Do not be anxious about anything, but in every situation, by prayer and petition, with thanksgiving, present your requests to God. And the peace of God, which transcends all understanding, will guard your hearts and your minds in Christ Jesus. Finally, brothers and sisters, whatever is true, whatever is noble, whatever is right, whatever is pure, whatever is lovely, whatever is admirable—if anything is excellent or praiseworthy—think about such things. Whatever you have learned or received or heard from me, or seen in me—put it into practice. And the God of peace will be with you* (Philippians 4:4–9 NIV).

Don't Be Ashamed of Me

One thing that I understood was that if I was going to get out of prison unscathed, it was only going to be by the grace of God, so I was not about to hide my faith from the other prisoners and I wasn't going to tarnish it in order to fit in with the crowd. The first thing that happened when I was shown to my bunk was that I opened my Bible, read a few verses, and prayed quietly to the Lord for a while.

I wanted to send a message to the other prisoners that this was who I was. Then I got up and walked through the place to check it over and look for a friendly face. A couple of guys invited me to join in on a cribbage game, so I sat down and they filled me in on the routine.

Food was brought in three times a day, and the tables we

were using for entertainment were also our dining tables. There was one TV with a couple of channels and a few benches for common viewing. When the weather was good, prisoners were allowed out in the exercise yard for a few hours each day. There was also the option twice a week to go to the gym for an hour or spend the same amount of time doing arts and crafts.

I was told that everyone eventually would be assigned to the laundry, the kitchen, or the tailor shop for four hours a day, and for that service everyone got a few dollars a day to save or to spend at the commissary for treats.

Once every two weeks, a Catholic priest would hold services in the chapel, and on the opposite Sunday the Protestants would hold their services. Lights-out was at ten o'clock, whether you liked it or not, and if you wanted breakfast you had to be up at six. Of course, there were the ever-present guards who were there night and day to keep things under control.

It wasn't long before the conversation turned to why I was in there. Everybody wants to know why everyone else is in prison, partly out of curiosity and partly to figure out where you fit in the prison hierarchy and class system. I told my story to my captive listeners whenever someone would ask. One thing that surprised me was the large number of inmates who were serving two years less a day just for alcohol-related charges.

It was a sobering thought when I contemplated that I had driven drunk many, many times in my early life. I was even caught a few times, but I had never been charged. I realized that for that crime alone, I deserved to be there just as much as any of those other men did, and I only had an eight-month sentence. It strengthened my resolve even more to find out why God wanted me to be there. Others were in there for theft or weapons offenses, or violence or sexual misconduct, and I had been guilty of all of those things at some time or other myself during my lifetime. Rather than complain about the time I did get, I considered myself fortunate that I was only facing an eight-month sentence.

Whenever someone tried to protest their innocence to me while I was in there, I pointed out to them that all of our sentences would be a lot longer if we had been convicted of all of the things that we did do and got away with it. I explained to them that the important thing was to just do the time and not go back into the same evil lifestyle again when we finally got out.

Fishing for Weeks and No Bites

The Bible tells us that some of Christ's disciples were originally fishermen. Then Jesus told them to follow Him, saying that He would make them fishers of men. Now there I was, fishing for souls in prison with hardly a nibble in weeks. Then one day, one of my cribbage partners confided that he would be getting out in a week. He had been in contact with some professing Christians before, both in and out of the joint, and he had never been impressed with them because they did not seem much different than he was.

But then he said he knew there was something different about me, and he really wanted what I had. He wanted to change his life when he got out, so for the next week, I took him through the basics of repentance and accepting Christ and I did my best to answer all of his questions about God and God's Word. The day that he left, he thanked me and told me that he was going to find a good church and start attending. Then he was gone, and the trouble started in earnest.

Satan Does Not Like to Lose Souls

Yes, I prayed and read my Bible every day in my cell, and I know full well that it was God's warriors (the angels of God) who were my ultimate protection while I was in prison, but I was not about to give the impression to anyone that I was going to be an easy target, either. I have had several years of martial arts training and I practiced my martial arts katas in my cell as a good way to keep in shape, as well as an advertisement to the other inmates that I was not to be messed with.

I was also quite strong for my size. In the weight room, I made sure that others were watching as I did leg presses with over four hundred pounds of weight on the other end. It was partly for exercise but partly to suggest to other individuals that maybe they should not try to cause trouble with me. However, there are lots of big, strong guys in prison, so you still need to be careful, and I knew that only God could guarantee my safety.

In addition, if you wanted to stir up a hornets' nest in your life, just start reaching out to people for Jesus. The devil hates that, and he will go to work to try to shut you up for good. There was one fellow in particular who did not like me. I was not concerned about him by himself because he had the demeanor of a coward, but once the fellow left to whom I had been witnessing, this other guy started stirring up some of the other prisoners and making threats against my life, saying that he and his friends were all going to "get me" one day.

In case you think that I am exaggerating the risk, BC Corrections Services data recorded over eight hundred inmate-on-inmate assaults at that particular prison during the six-year period between 2004 and 2006, and seventy assaults against staff during the same time period. I prayed to the Lord about what to do at the time, and I felt assured that I had been faithful to God and the man that I was supposed to talk to was now gone, so I went to let the warden know what was going on and he agreed to transfer me into the maximum-security wing of the prison.

In the maximum-security wing where I was now headed, one of the inmates had just been reintegrated back into the wing after a week in isolation for seriously assaulting another inmate and all privileges had been temporarily revoked until things settled down again. Prison is no joke, my friends. It's a dangerous place. Be wiser than I was. If you have not been living for God, start now. Trust me. You will not enjoy prison.

Maximum-Security Prison Is No Picnic

When you look at things from a natural perspective, this might seem like it was going from the frying pan into the fire. This was where all the high-risk offenders were housed. There were murderers and violent offenders and sexual offenders just waiting to be remanded to federal prison for their long-term sentences.

There were people with psychotic problems who wandered around muttering to themselves for a good part of the day. One fellow in particular would often pace back and forth in the common area, jabbering to himself or to some unseen spiritual tormentor. Suddenly, he would just stop, stare someone in the eye, and declare, "I would rather burn than fade away!" and then he would resume his pacing and babbling. Then there were other people who were there for their own protection, because, for whatever reasons, they were not safe in the general population.

In spite of the seriousness of the crimes of some of these inmates, everyone was actually somewhat safer in the maximum-security wing, because security was a lot tighter there. There were more guard checks, and one guard was always stationed just outside the door of the common area to keep an eye on things. There were less privileges, though. You only got one hour of exercise time a day, and there were two prisoners per one eight-by-ten cell that was locked from ten at night till six in the morning.

All of that meant that you had better hope that you got along with your cellmate in maximum security because you were locked in there with them for eight hours every night. If you had a good cellmate, you were actually safer at night than in the general population. But if not, things could go badly for you before the guard ever got to you. I think they have toilets in the cells now, but they did not when I was there. If you had to use the washroom during the night, too bad for you. If you were desperate enough, there was a steel bucket under your bed that you could use. Then you would get the privilege of washing it out yourself the next morning if you had to use it during the night.

To give you an idea of how small these cells were, the beds took up half the space. That left about four feet by ten feet for two people. That was only four steps from one end of the cell to the other, and there was hardly enough room to walk past each other if you were both standing up in the cell at the same time. There was nothing to do in the cell but sit or lie on your bed day or night. You couldn't even read at night, because there were no lights allowed after ten.

Friendly Faces in Hard Places

The moment I first entered the cell block, I was surprised to see a familiar friendly face from my home church. He was a genuinely nice guy who had professed to be a Christian, but he was a person of diminished mental capacity. I found out later that he had gotten himself in trouble due to the dangerous combination of his adult sexual urges combined with his mental deficiencies and the moral compass of a preschooler.

I had always treated him kindly on the outside, so he was really glad to see me and he offered to let me have the empty bunk in his cell. There wasn't any other choice anyway. It was the only empty bunk in the whole wing. The guy was eager to have some friendly company, so I was happy to bunk with him, although I wondered why the only spare bed was in his cell when all the other cells were full. Overcrowding was obviously a problem in maximum security, as well as in the general population, and I was fortunate to get a bed there at all, but I wondered why such a friendly guy didn't have a cellmate.

We talked for hours about why I was there and why he was there, and I strongly encouraged him in simple terms that we both had to repent and live our lives completely for Jesus so that we would never have to come back to a place like this again. We read my Bible and prayed together until lights-out. About ten minutes later, I found out why this guy had no cellmate. He snored like somebody revving a motorcycle with no baffles in the muffler, and he did it all night long.

When this fellow was sleeping, you could clearly hear him all the way at the other end of the cell block, and now I was stuck with him in an eight-by-ten steel speaker box every night for eight hours a night. I hardly slept at all for the first two days, until someone else was released and I was able to move into a cell with another professing Christian about halfway down the cell block. Then the next newbie would have to go through the initiation of trying to sleep in the other cell with the snoring cellmate. Fortunately, my former cellmate was understanding about why I had to move, and we remained good friends throughout my stay there.

Professing Christians in Prison

It might surprise you to know that there are actually quite a few Christians in prison. Some become Christians while they are in there, but the majority are there because they were never taught repentance as an essential component of their salvation. They thought that they would be able to claim that Jesus is Lord with their lips and still live for the devil in their daily behavior, and now there they were, in prison, paying for their foolishness.

I was determined that before I left the prison, I would do whatever I could to change things for the better in there. I was also committed to the goal that by the time I left, there would not be any professing Christian in that prison who was under the false impression that you could keep on sinning and still go to heaven.

As with the general population wing, I never tried to push Christianity on anybody, but anyone interested was able to hear the unfiltered story of how I ended up in prison and how God had changed my life. Word gets around quickly in prison. Before long, I found out that the maximum-security population of fifty inmates contained about a half-dozen professing Christians and a few more who were open to hearing about Christianity. They were all like sheep without a shepherd, and they looked to me to help them.

The Christian prisoners asked if I would be willing to set up a half-hour daily Bible study and teaching time for anyone who wanted to attend. I was happy to do so, focusing mainly on repentance, faith in Jesus Christ, and the other fundamentals of salvation and Christian discipleship. By focusing on the fundamentals of salvation, I labored to ensure that all who listened and believed would have the best opportunity of success when they left prison, through having a solid base of repentance and faith in the rock of Jesus Christ upon which to build their lives. Thanks to these Bible studies and my witnessing, during my time there I was able to lead two people to accept Jesus Christ as their Savior, and I believe that many more were influenced toward thinking about God and salvation.

Physical Hardships and Social Security

I found the steel prison bunks with almost no padding very hard on my back, which made it difficult to sleep sometimes, and that was further complicated by the fact that I had injured my ribs playing volleyball one day during exercise time. Injured ribs are something that takes three or four weeks to heal, and the doctors can't really do much to help it along.

For a while, I was so sore that I could not even sit up to get out of bed. I had to roll over, drop my feet off the edge, and sort of push myself to a standing position using my leg muscles and my arms. There was nothing that could be done about it other than to wait for them to heal on their own, but for a while, even coughing or sneezing was agony for me, and that steel bunk did not help matters at all.

On the other hand, I found that in the maximum-security wing, even the non-Christian inmates were easier to get along with than those in the general population. It turned out that the inmates had a lot of respect for me because I was honest and transparent with everyone, not like the phony Christians whom they were used to encountering. Over time, opportunities arose to talk with many of these troubled men about the things of God.

There was one big first nations fellow who stood out from all the others, and I mean it literally. He was about six-foot-four and three hundred pounds, and he was in the maximum-security wing on remand awaiting transfer to the federal prison for an alcohol-related triple murder. This was the guy who had just returned from solitary confinement after putting the hurt on a fellow prisoner just a few days before I had arrived. As far as I knew, he was the biggest guy in the whole place, and for some reason, he took a liking to me. I believe that God gave me favor with him.

We had a lot of spare time in prison, so we'd often play a variety of board games as we talked. This guy would complain and throw a tantrum sometimes when he lost, but I think that he respected that I wasn't really afraid of him, and consequently I would not let him win whatever game we were playing all the time. I'm pretty sure that he would have had my back if anyone had tried anything against me, particularly while I was nursing my injured ribs.

I socialized with this man a lot, talking about life and God while I was in there. He never accepted Christ, but we spent a lot of social time together, and I was pretty grateful that God had given me a wingman who was built like the famous wrestler Andre the Giant. Besides, who knows what might come of it all in the end? He was looking at the possibility of life in prison for his sins, but maybe in the end I'll see him in heaven. I hope so.

Working for Christ in the Prison System

I was determined to do more than just serve my time while I was in prison. I firmly believed that the Lord had put me there for a reason, so I looked for any opportunities to make positive changes wherever that was possible. I had noticed that the Catholic priest appeared to be a very devout man who was genuinely concerned about the spiritual welfare of the inmates. In addition to his services every second Sunday, he also spent a lot of quality time encouraging the men during the week.

I was not very happy about the idea of only experiencing church every second Sunday, so I asked the priest if he would mind if the Protestant inmates also attended his Sunday services. He was a pretty open-minded guy, and he was so thrilled with the idea that when we all showed up, he would loan me his guitar and allow me to lead the praise and worship part of the service.

I don't know whether the practice of attending services every week continued after I left, but I hope that it did. I am far less concerned about a little Catholic tradition rubbing off on an inmate than I am about a prisoner going to hell because no one ever warned them that they had to repent and accept Jesus as their Savior.

The other thing that concerned me about the prison system at that time was that there was a library that contained books with plenty of novels about violence and questionable sexual morality, and even more than a few horror novels, but there were only a few Bibles and virtually no solid Christian reading material. After talking with the warden, I obtained permission to phone back to some friends in Kelowna and have them bring up a big stack of Christian books for the library in order to help the inmates learn more about Christianity and about how to grow in their faith in God.

Up for Parole

In the Canadian correctional system, unless there are extenuating circumstances, once an inmate has served a third of his sentence, he becomes eligible for parole, but it is certainly no guarantee that he will be let out. When I was brought before the parole board, I did not really expect to make parole. Some serious crimes had recently been committed by other parolees, and there was a great deal of political pressure being applied to try to tighten up the parole system. Considering the seriousness of the charges against me and the fact that very few paroles were going through at the time, things did not look very optimistic for me.

After the meeting with the parole officers was over, they asked me to wait outside while they held a private discussion. When I was called back in, I was a little shocked to hear their decision. After serving only three months of my sentence, I was going to be released on probation for two years. During that period of time, I would have to report regularly to a probation officer and attend psychological counseling. After that, I would be a free man.

The parole officers wished me luck and expressed that they hoped that they would never see me in there again. It took another few days to take care of the paperwork, and then suddenly I was a free man. I said my good-byes to everyone on the inside and then was escorted out of the facility. I was free.

When they booked me out, I was grateful to see that some Christian friends had showed up on my release date to give me a ride back home. Looking back on it now, I think that one of the reasons I got the early parole was that the devil just wanted me out of there before I did any further damage to his kingdom.

23

Return to Public Ministry

God Restores My Life

I have never regretted or resented God for requiring me to go to prison for a time. The truth is that I deserved to be there as much as anyone else who was there, and being required to pay my debt to society for at least some of my sins has helped me to achieve closure on that part of my life.

It was also in prison that I had the honor of leading two people to accept Jesus Christ as their Savior. Before that time, I had witnessed to many people about accepting Christ over the years. I had directed seekers to churches and other church leaders, who then led them to accept Jesus, but it was not until I went to prison that I personally was able to lead anyone to accept Jesus Christ as their Savior, and that is a precious memory to me.

Upon returning to the outside, it was a bit of a shock to me when a few professing Christians distanced themselves from me and treated me coldly and unkindly at first when I got out. False rumors were circulated by those who did not know the whole story, rumors that were instrumental in generating an atmosphere of fear and mistrust among those who chose to believe them, but the Lord assured me that these rifts would be healed in time as long as I remained faithful to Him.

Far more Christians were kind and helpful to me as I set out on my new life for God, now unhindered by the chains of my past. One of the stipulations of my parole was that I had to have a supervised place to stay until my parole was over. A faithful retired Christian couple rented me their basement suite until the requirements of my parole were complete and I was finally free to live on my own.

Being required to visit a secular psychologist and report to the parole officer was inconvenient and a little frustrating because of their ungodly philosophies and perspectives on life, but I chose to look at it again as an opportunity to witness to two more people about how Jesus Christ had changed my life and how I was no longer the same person that I used to be. I even continued to keep in contact with the parole officer for several years afterward regarding ongoing rehabilitation Christian counseling that I was doing to help young offenders and adults who were going through some of the same things that I had gone through.

My former pastor in Kelowna welcomed me back into his fellowship, where I gladly sat and ministered under his leadership for many years. There was also the Christian organization that, in spite of my past, sponsored me for my ministry license and ordination. Then the Christian Minister's Association accepted me as a pastoral member. Since that time, I have ministered in different ways in numerous different locations, sometimes as a senior pastor and sometimes as an associate pastor. Not once have I ever desired to go back to my former life.

God Is All I Need

One of the greatest challenges that I have ever had to face in my life is loneliness. From my early youth, I had always wanted to love and be loved and share my life with someone, but Satan used pornography and my own sexual lust to steal that from me. As a young man, I thought that the solution to my loneliness was to find a wife and raise a family, but that did not solve the problem.

I have since learned that without God, there is a hole in our lives that cannot be filled with anything else but Him. Wealth and fame cannot fill it. Marriage and children cannot fill it. Yet evil will find a way into that hole in our lives if we allow it to enter, and then evil will work toward destroying us.

Once I truly understood that I was created by God to love and be loved by Him, the Holy Spirit started pushing the evil and the loneliness out of that hole in my life. I realized that God was all I really needed to experience a joyous and fulfilling life on earth until Jesus returns or until I pass on to heaven before that day.

I finally reached a place of contentment in my life—believing that if it was God's will for me to remain single for the rest of my life, I would be happy with that. No matter what, I came to the peaceful realization that for the rest of my life, I only wanted to continue to serve the Lord.

> *My son, do not forget my teaching, but keep my commands in your heart, for they will prolong your life many years and bring you peace and prosperity. Let love and faithfulness never leave you; bind them around your neck, write them on the tablet of your heart. Then you will win favor and a good name in the sight of God and man. Trust in the Lord with all your heart and lean not on your own understanding; in all your ways submit to him, and he will make your paths straight. Do not be wise in your own eyes; fear the Lord and*

shun evil. This will bring health to your body and nourishment to your bones (Proverbs 3:1–8 NIV).

Ever since my conversion in 1981, the main focus of my life has been to take what God has given to me and pass it on to others. I work at a secular job to put food on the table and a roof over our heads, but I live to tell other people about Jesus Christ in the hope that through my testimony and my teaching, God will be gracious and save others, as well.

God Restored What Satan Had Stolen

Then one day, God also gave me an added blessing to my life by the name of Leigh Ann. Nine years after I met her, God opened my eyes to view this precious and beautiful young woman, whom I had seen in Kelowna on the first day of Bible college, in a new and different way. From the very beginning, I had noticed that she embodied the wonderful, gentle spirit of a godly woman, and we had become close friends over the years. Leigh Ann wrote to me when I was in prison. She encouraged me to continue to have faith, and her letters had greatly blessed me during that time.

Leigh Ann was also at my mother's side holding her hand when Mom passed on to be with Jesus. As I watched my mom's spirit fade away and head for the glories of heaven in 1994, the Lord said, "This is the wife whom I have chosen for you." We were married that same year, and she has been my constant companion now for over twenty years. We both know that God is our Father and that we are His children, and our journey back to the Father God is almost complete.

> *God, my shepherd! I don't need a thing. You have bedded me down in lush meadows, you find me quiet pools to drink from. True to your word, you let me catch my breath and send me in the right direction. Even when the way goes through the Valley of Death, I'm not afraid when you walk at my side. Your trusty shepherd's crook makes me feel secure. You serve me a six-course dinner right in front of my enemies. You revive my drooping head; my cup brims with blessing. Your beauty and love chase after me every day of my life. I'm back home in the house of God for the rest of my life* (Psalm 23 MSG).

I love God. He is my true Father in heaven, and I would not trade my relationship with Jesus Christ for anything this world has to offer. I am looking forward to His coming, and I want to go with Him when He comes back to this earth to take us to our heavenly home. I have one desire in this world that is above all other things, dear reader, and that is the hope that when I get to heaven, you too will be there.

24

The Way of Salvation

Would You Like to Receive Jesus Christ as Your Savior?

This is my first book. I believe that there will be others, but this book will not be complete if I do not pass on the opportunity for every reader to receive the wonderful gift of eternal life that God has given to us through repentance and faith in Jesus Christ as our Savior.

God's Word tells us that our Father God is a loving, forgiving, and merciful God, who does not condemn us. The whole world is condemned already, due to the evil that is inherent in humanity as a result of Adam's choice to welcome evil into our human nature. God's desire is to save us from this state of eternal servitude to Satan in which mankind presently exists.

For this purpose, the Father God sent His only begotten, sinless Son, Jesus Christ, to earth to take the penalty for our sin upon Himself. Jesus Christ willingly submitted to death on the cross to pay the penalty for Adam's mistake, to pay the penalty for all of mankind's sins. For that selfless act of love, the Father God raised Jesus Christ from the grave to immortality, and He has declared Him to be the Savior of the entire world. Jesus Christ is the fulfilment of God's promise to the first two human beings—Adam and Eve—that one day one of Eve's descendants would become the Redeemer of the human race, offering salvation to all who choose to turn from evil and accept Jesus as their Savior.

Do You Want Assurance That You Are Saved?

Many people in the world today live in fear of God and in fear of the coming judgment because of ongoing sin in their lives, but it does not have to be that way. God has shown us the path to salvation and all we have to do is take it. Just repent. Stop doing evil. Depart from iniquity and accept Jesus Christ as our Savior, choosing instead to walk in obedience to Jesus Christ.

> *"Enter through the narrow gate. For wide is the gate and broad is the road that leads to destruction, and many enter through it. But small is the gate and narrow the road that leads to life, and only a few find it.... Not everyone who says to me, 'Lord, Lord,' will enter the kingdom of heaven, but only the one who does the will of my Father who is in heaven. Many will say to me on that day, 'Lord, Lord, did we not prophesy in your name and in your name drive out demons and in your name perform many miracles?' Then I will tell them plainly, 'I never knew you. Away from me, you evildoers!' Therefore everyone who hears these words of mine and puts them into practice is like a wise man who built his house on the rock. The rain came down, the streams rose, and the winds blew and beat against that house; yet it did not fall, because it had its foundation on the rock. But everyone who hears these words of mine and does not put them into practice is like a foolish man who built his house on sand.*

The rain came down, the streams rose, and the winds blew and beat against that house, and it fell with a great crash" (Matthew 7:13–27 NIV).

I strongly urge you with tears not to let your house collapse as I once did. God promises us that the way to salvation is not complicated. It is so simple that even a small child can understand it. All that God asks of us is that we reject—repent from—the evil thoughts, speech, and behavior in our lives and accept Jesus as our Savior.

We are all prodigal sons and daughters. All God wants for us to do is turn away from darkness and turn back to Him so that we can be a part of His family again. God promises that if we repent and accept Jesus Christ as our Savior, God will give us the opportunity to receive His Holy Spirit to empower and help us to live our lives in a way that is pleasing to God. That's all there is to it. That's what it means to be "born again" by the Spirit of God.

Accept God's Help!

The reason I stress the importance of being so willing to receive the Holy Spirit is that God does not want you to go through the trials of life and the struggles against sin on your own. Some of you have probably tried to do that many times by yourself and failed over and over again, just like I once did. That's not the way it has to be. There is victory for you. God wants to help you to overcome sin and be victorious over Satan. Receive the Holy Spirit and let Him help you!

God's Word tells us that if we have repented of our sins and accepted Jesus Christ as our Savior, we are spiritually born again. We are saved, but there is more to Christianity than just being saved. Just as natural children need adults to love and care for them, to protect them, to guide them, and to help them grow into maturity, so do those who are newly born again in the Spirit. We need help and protection and the loving nurture and oversight of good Christian leaders if we are to grow into strong, healthy, mature Christians ourselves.

Don't avoid or forsake attending a good Bible-believing church. True Christians know that going to church doesn't save us. We participate in Christian services because we believe God when He says that it will be beneficial for us. We acknowledge that God has anointed leaders in the Church to help us learn the meaning and value of water baptism and communion. We know that God has put His Church here on this earth to teach us about Him, along with the Holy Spirit and His gifts. We know they are there to help us grow and mature and bring us back to the Holy Spirit's path of righteousness whenever we stray from it.

Don't try to be a Christian all on your own. That's as abnormal as the thought of a newborn infant rejecting all contact from his parents who want to feed and help him and love him and protect him from harm. Learn to trust the Word of God when it says that it is good for us to meet together regularly for corporate teaching, for worship, for prayer and fellowship.

God is our Father in heaven. He has provided loving surrogate parents for us in the form of Bible-believing pastors and other mature Christians. The Bible tells us that they are the shepherds of God's flocks. God has called them to take care of us and help us grow until we are mature enough to also bring others to the Lord with a solid foundation of the Gospel of Jesus Christ.

Let's all work together toward that goal. Then, when Jesus

comes for His bride, we will all clearly see the open door to heaven and enter in. Who in their right mind would want to find out the truth later by trying to get Jesus to reopen the door, only to have Him say, "I do not know you. Depart from Me, you evildoers and all of you who work iniquity."

My dear readers, we are at the midnight hour in the clock of human history. God is raising up prophets to warn Christianity that we are in the end times. There are many who are blind and unconcerned about sin in the Church, thinking that Jesus will overlook it all because we profess that "Jesus is Lord." If that is what you have believed, you have believed a lie, another false gospel.

This book is only a small part of a cry that is beginning to go out worldwide to all who profess to know Jesus Christ as the Savior. In the parable of the ten virgins, they are all looking for the coming of the Bridegroom, but Jesus said that five of them were wise and five of them were foolish. The wise will go with Jesus when He returns for His bride. The foolish will be left behind to share the fate of the rest of those who have lived wickedly.

God wants us all of us to be wise and walking in the light when Jesus returns. I pray that the love of God, the obedient example of Jesus Christ, and the peace and joy of the Holy Spirit will guide you into all truth. Then, if we are all still alive when the time comes, this Scripture will become a reality:

But let me tell you something wonderful, a mystery I'll probably never fully understand. We're not all going to die—but we are all going to be changed. You hear a blast to end all blasts from a trumpet, and in the time that you look up and blink your eyes—it's over. On signal from that trumpet from heaven, the dead will be up and out of their graves, beyond the reach of death, never to die again. At the same moment and in the same way, we'll all be changed. In the resurrection scheme of things, this has to happen: everything perishable taken off the shelves and replaced by the imperishable, this mortal replaced by the immortal. Then the saying will come true:

> *Death swallowed by triumphant Life! Who got the last word, oh, Death? Oh, Death, who's afraid of you now? It was sin that made death so frightening and law-code guilt that gave sin its leverage, its destructive power. But now in a single victorious stroke of Life, all three—sin, guilt, death—are gone, the gift of our Master, Jesus Christ. Thank God! With all this going for us, my dear, dear friends, stand your ground. And don't hold back. Throw yourselves into the work of the Master, confident that nothing you do for him is a waste of time or effort* (1 Corinthians 15:54–58 MSG).

Sincerely,
Your true friend and servant of Jesus Christ,
Michael Hunter

About the Author

PASTOR MICHAEL HUNTER has been involved in teaching and prophetic ministry for more than thirty years. Michael served for eight years as founding member and board member of National Missionary Evangelistic Association, a Christian ministry, which focused on exposing the harmful effects of pornography, helping victims of abuse, and counselling and rehabilitation of criminal offenders. He served for five years with Chariot Ministries as speaker and vocalist, providing public outreach ministry in preaching and music to various communities throughout the Okanagan area of British Columbia. He has been a member of the Christian Ministers Association of Canada since 1987. Michael presently functions as associate pastor at Lake Country Life Center in British Columbia, where he currently ministers, as well as being a guest speaker at other local ministries.

Contact Information

The author can be reached at 1-250-762-8605
or email him at mhunter1@telus.net.